The Collective Potential

A Holistic Approach to Managing
Information Flow in Collaborative
Design and Construction Environments

Andreas Floros Phelps

*To all those who have shown me the great
potential of this world and made me
believe that it is within reach.*

Contents

Introduction

Information is the basis for everything that we do. It is what allows us to make sense of our surroundings. It is what enables us to make decisions regarding how to act and how to respond to our environment. It is the foundation for every activity that we endeavor to take on. As human beings, however, we are rationally bounded; that is, we can process only a limited amount of information.

In order to overcome this limitation, we work together and use information to communicate with each other, coordinate our efforts, and realize outcomes that transcend our individual limitations. As we take on more complex and challenging activities and try to execute them faster and with greater precision, the effective management of the flow of information becomes even more critical to our success.

For all its importance, however, there is very little understanding of what is meant by "information flow", or "information", for that matter. In recent years, there have been scores of books about collaboration, knowledge management, and information management, and countless technical programs, processes, and strategies aimed at improving information flow. Despite all these efforts, there is still very little understanding of the underlying phenomenon of information flowing from one person to another in large short-term collaborative teams.

This knowledge gap regarding the science of information flow first became abundantly clear to me during my first few years as a building technology consultant working with architects, building owners, and contractors in the area of building science and technology (i.e. how a building performs). I spent those first couple of years learning as much as I could and trying to package that knowledge in such a way that others could easily understand it and make use of it. I naively thought that good information and ideas that "just made sense" should just be accepted instantly and universally. Although there was significant potential value in the work products I was turning out, it seemed to me that only a relatively small portion of the information I was sharing with others was getting incorporated into the project and resulting in actual value; most of the information just seemed to be lost somewhere in the process.

In construction, there are dozens of different types of consultants, engineers, designers, contractors, and manufacturers involved with each project. If the types of information inefficiencies I was experiencing held true for others on the project team, then there was a tremendous amount of potential value that was simply getting lost. In my conversations with other building professionals, it became clear that they too felt that their knowledge contributions were not being used to their full potential. Most seemed to accept this as part of the nature of the building industry, but there were some who continuously sought more effective means of getting their clients to better understand and incorporate their knowledge contributions.

What I began to realize was that regardless of how good an idea is, if it can't be effectively communicated to those who are expected to carry it out, it may never add any true value. For my part, I focused on the world of contractors, who I viewed as the people who ultimately take the ideas of the designers and translate them into reality. This led me to pursue a doctorate in construction management at the Pennsylvania State University where I spent several years trying to understand the phenomenon of what happens to the information shared within multi-disciplinary project teams engaged in complex, short-term collaboration.

While at Penn State, I had the good fortune of interacting not only with the architectural engineering department, but also some of the great minds in the business school and one of the few information science professors interested in socio-technical processes. Their combined influence gave me a very unique perspective from which to understand the construction industry.

My research involved three years of in-depth observations of a project team charged with delivering a cancer research center and a children's hospital at a major medical center. Over the next three years, I sat in on hundreds of meetings and had countless informal conversations with various project team members to try to understand their thoughts, feelings, and behaviors related to the information they were responsible for sharing, as well as how they felt about the information shared by others. By collecting these data, coding them, and conducting different types of analyses, certain themes emerged related to information behavior. Based on these initial themes, subsequent observations allowed me to refine these themes and link them to create a theory of information flow. The beauty of this type of ethnographic study is that since the theory is developed from and continuously refined by observations of an actual project team, the theory is grounded in reality and more directly applicable to practice. What emerged from this study was a relatively simple relationship between information sharing, trust, and learning that is arguably the most critical factor in the success of information flow within teams. However, along the way to developing this theory, there were numerous additional valuable insights related to understanding the characteristics of information, the structure of information flow, and the major moderators of information flow. These insights into the social and technical aspects of information flow provide the basis for developing a detailed understanding of how we can more effectively manage information flow on our projects and set the basis for understanding the science behind integration.

One of the most unique aspects of this research was that it was not developed from abstractions of theory, but instead emerged from observing real project teams on real projects dealing with real issues. This "grounded theory" approach is based on the assumption that the truth is already there in front of us, but that through detailed analysis we can sift through the complexity and confusion to realize the elegantly simple explanation that has always been there. An analogy that often comes to my mind is of the Renaissance artist Michelangelo. It was said that when he was selecting a block of marble for a sculpture, he would make his decision based on the form that he felt was already trapped within the marble. Thus, his job as a sculptor was not to create, but to free the form that already exists trapped in the block of stone. His responsibility as an artist was to understand the properties and characteristics of the block of marble, its behaviors and tendencies, its limitations and sensitivities, and work in concert with all these things so that he could gradually free the form trapped inside. By removing the burden of unnecessary and distracting excesses, he could allow the intrinsic value of what had always been there to realize its full potential.

Building upon the findings of my doctoral research, the intent of this book is to provide a means of understanding information flow so that managers can not only methodically plan out information flow on projects, but also navigate and adapt their plan to respond to changing conditions. With a focus on both the social and technical aspects of collaboration, the concepts presented in this book explain why certain competencies, tools, technologies, and processes result in more effective information flow than others. As John Tarpey, Regional CEO of Balfour Beatty Construction's Northern Division, commented, "this work explains what we experience every day, only now we have a means of understanding it,

4

analyzing it, planning for it, and using it to improve future outcomes."

This book is organized similarly to the process by which these concepts were developed, specifically: 1) understanding the details and characteristics of all the different components involved with information flow; 2) understanding the interactions between those components and the resulting phenomena; and finally 3) applying this understanding to the tools, processes, and behaviors that we use in practice. Each chapter is essential to understanding the subsequent chapters. As these initially disparate ideas become more and more tightly woven together, they begin to provide some powerful insight into how the construction industry currently behaves and how we can better tap into the tremendous potential that already exists. John Tocci of Tocci Building Corporation summed it up best by saying "this book develops several important yet seemingly separate concepts and forces the reader to hold them suspended in space. Then, all of a sudden, they snap into place with the assembly becoming hugely meaningful."

The first half of the book focuses on the science behind information flow and integration. While the first four chapters are more theoretical in nature, they provide the needed background knowledge to apply these concepts in practice. Chapters five through seven discuss how these concepts can be used in practice. A brief description of each chapter follows:

Chapter 1, *The Structure of Information Flow*, outlines the basic components of information flow and describes in detail the social and technical characteristics of each component. There is a lot of information condensed into this chapter, but it is necessary foundation for thinking in terms of the socio-technical nature of information flow. It also sets up the basis for understanding how these components interplay to influence the flow of information in collaborative teams.

Chapter 2, *Trust, Commitment, Learning, and Understanding,* discusses the major moderators of information flow and reviews relevant academic and nonacademic publications related to these topics. These four constructs are vital to understanding the intellectual, psychological, and sociological processes that influence team information behaviors.

Chapter 3, *Trust and Learning Cycles,* presents the major conceptual contribution of this work. It describes how the four moderators described in Chapter 2 are interrelated and intimately depend on how information is shared. It describes how cycles of trust and learning continuously interact with each other in virtuous or vicious cycles to either improve or worsen information flow and describes certain behaviors can trigger or change these trends. These concepts are summarized in a conceptual model that can be used to understand and analyze project team interactions and can ultimately be used to plan and manage information flow.

Chapter 4, *Decision Making and Ambiguity,* describes how the intellectual and emotional shifts described in Chapter 3 are critical to effective decision-making. Although these shifts can only be brought about through conflict, the type of conflict strongly influences the direction of the change. This chapter reviews basic theoretical constructs related to conflict and outlines important role that ambiguity plays in determining the type of conflict and presents a hierarchy of ambiguity model that explains the different types of ambiguity and how they need to be managed in order to facilitate positive shifts in commitment and understanding.

Chapter 5, *Information Flow Management,* looks at how the concepts discussed in Chapters 3 and 4 can be applied to information flow planning over an entire project. By tying together these concepts with components of lean production management and process mapping, this chapter ties together the concepts of the previous chapters and reformulates them in terms of how certain competencies, tools, and processes should be integrated into an overall process map to develop a holistic information flow management plan.

Chapter 6, *Managing the Project Team Culture*, is a basic overview of the tensions and synergies between organizational strategy and structure and their fit to the market environment. In addition to providing a general overview of classic organizational structures and strategies, it also describes the unique situation of construction project teams. By applying these fundamental organizational science concepts to the domain of construction teams, this chapter discusses the important structural, strategic, and environmental considerations needed to create environments best suited for the development of trust and learning and subsequently improved information flow.

Chapter 7, *The Path Forward*, places the concepts presented in the earlier chapters within the context of certain major industry trends (i.e. sustainable design, building information modeling, and integrated project delivery). It also challenges our industries and academic institutions to place more of a focus on information flow management and related topics. Finally, it paints an idyllic picture of how project teams could function and a hope that the industry is on its way to realizing that ideal.

––––––––

My hope is that the information in this book will help to elevate information flow planning to a science and practice so that we can effectively use our knowledge and truly realize the greatness of our collective potential.

Chapter 1:

The Structure of Information Flow

In order for there to be flow of any type, it's necessary to have five basic components: 1) a flow substance; 2) a starting point; 3) an ending point; 4) a path between the two points; and 5) a driving force. A simple example is that of water through a pipe. The purpose of the pipe is to move water from one point to another. Flow in this type of system depends on the characteristics of: 1) the water (the substance); 2) the source of the water (the start point); 3) the destination of the water (the end point); 4) the piping system itself (the path); and 5) the forces acting upon the system, such as gravity, pumps, or some other means (the driving force).

For information flow in project teams, the primary concern is getting valuable information to flow between people and other technical objects so that it can eventually contribute value to the project. The basic components that make up the underlying structure for information flow are: 1) the information itself (the substance); 2) sources of information (the start points); 3) receivers of information (the end points); 4) interactions (the path); and 5) mutual relevance, or the alignment of information needs with available information (the driving force). Each of these components has specific characteristics that influence the effectiveness of their role in information flow. Understanding these components and their social and technical characteristics is fundamental to effectively managing information flow.

The Substance: Information and Information Types

In any construction project, there are three major flows that need to be considered: materials, labor, and information. In project teams, it is easier to focus on labor and material flows because they are tangible and more easily understood. However, the flow of information is what enables and provides the basis for these other flows. The characteristics of labor and material flows are, in most cases, relatively well understood (e.g. technical specifications of equipment, usage rates, waste factors, production rates, etc.). This allows us to analyze, plan, and manage these flows. However, we have an extremely poor understanding of the characteristics of information and information flow. Since information is what enables all labor and material flows, this presents a significant and pervasive problem for the design and construction industry.

As a point of clarification, it is important to understand the semantic difference between "data", "information", and "knowledge". Mark Nissen (2006a) makes the important distinction that these terms lie on a spectrum (see Figure 1). At one end is "data" that are highly abundant but have low actionability (i.e. ability to be used for direct action). At the other end of the spectrum is "knowledge" that has low abundance but high actionability. "Information" lies in the middle of the spectrum. Therefore, the communication of knowledge requires that an person #1 translate their abstract knowledge (e.g. how the color of a building's roof influences building energy efficiency) into information (e.g. the reflectance of a white roof is 90%) that is communicated with data (e.g. "roof", "reflectance", "90%"). The data then have to be observed by person #2 (i.e. heard or seen), understood and turned back into information, and then internalized as knowledge so that person #2 can apply it to the specific situation.

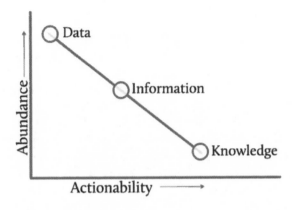

Figure 1: Characterization of Data, Information, and Knowledge

When we impart our knowledge to others, there are varying levels of complexity that the information can have. An easy means of understanding information complexity is to consider how easily it can be captured or codified. Codifying information is the process of capturing information into some sort of explicit form so that it can be easily transmitted to others (e.g. capturing information from a person's knowledge base and putting it into the form of reports, sketches, models, etc). Michael Polanyi was the first to make the important distinction between explicit and tacit knowledge (1966); explicit knowledge being knowledge that can be articulated in formal language (e.g. through words, numbers, formulae, etc.) and easily captured in reports, drawings, or some other type of *boundary object* (i.e. an information artifact that is used to transfer information across organizational, geographical, or temporal boundaries). Tacit knowledge, on the other hand, is knowledge that has slowly been accumulated through experience and is intertwined with personal beliefs, perspectives, instincts, and values. Because of its complexity, the full meaning of tacit knowledge is difficult to accurately convey to others. There is also a third type of information, implicit information, which consists of information that could easily be codified but has not been (Nissen, 2006b). In unique projects, there will always be a need for the valuable tacit knowledge provided by experienced professionals. However, there is significant value that can be gained by effectively codifying implicit information so that it can be more easily shared and built upon collaboratively. To do this requires the right types of boundary objects, competencies, and processes, and will be discussed in greater detail in the following sections.

Another way to characterize information is by its scope and content type. Information's scope is primarily defined by the entity providing it and their contractual role (e.g. mechanical designer, sustainability consultant, plumber, roofer, elevator manufacturer). The information that they need to conduct their work or that results from their work is part of their scope. Content type is more general and includes: 1) *design-related information* (e.g. material, systems, layout, and orientation); 2) *construction-related information* (e.g. means and methods, schedule, and cost); 3) *performance-related information* (e.g. the design intent, standard of care, or basis for design); and 4) *strategy-related information* (e.g. overall planning, major milestones, and contractual relationships). In addition to these four, there are two other content types that are not usually thought of, but make up 30-60% of information shared in team discussions (see Figure 2). These are: 5) *administrative information* (e.g. related to formal processes, approvals, and protocols); and 6) *informal communication information* (e.g. who is responsible for developing a sketch, when it will be available, who will get manufacturer feedback).

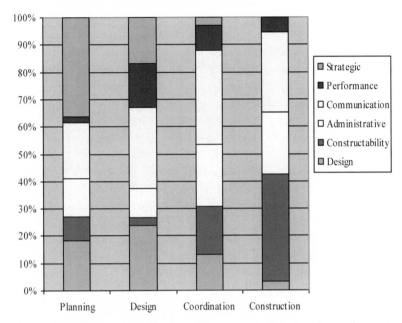

Figure 2: Information Content Types and Relative Prevalence in Construction Phases

Information can also be categorized by its level of abstraction. Within a specific scope, information goes from being very abstract to very concrete as the project progresses. At the beginning, the focus is on *the intent* of a specific scope or work. Based on the intent, information is used to develop 2) a *product description* and 3) a *process description*. Then as the project progresses, then there is information about 4) the *implementation* of the work. Finally, as the work is completed, there is information related to 5) *conformance/verification* regarding how well the completed work met the descriptions and the intent.

For example, the design of a building's exterior cladding starts with a basis of design that outlines the performance requirements (i.e. intent). The architect has guidelines for how the drawings and specifications should be organized (i.e. product description) and a general process for design development (i.e. a process description). As the actual design progresses (i.e. implementation), there are reviews and analyses (i.e. verification) that can be conducted to make sure that the final product will meet the intent. The final product, i.e. the drawings and specification, then provide the intent for the construction phase.

These different ways of thinking about information are an important starting point when planning and managing information flows. Codifiability influences the level of reliance on people versus boundary objects. Scope and content type influence the types of people and references that should be involved. Abstractness influences how information should be ordered and linked. As with any other type of flow, the more that is understood about the characteristics of the substance, the better we can predict how it will behave with respect to its interaction with different sources, receivers, paths, and driving forces.

Sources and Receivers of Information:
People and Boundary Objects

For information flow to occur, two things need to happen. The information needs to be made available (by an information source) and then be accepted (by an information receiver). Within projects, there are two main types of information sources and receivers: people and boundary objects. These two types provide important complementary roles. People (i.e. project team members) are best suited to provide tacit and implicit information and play a vital role in terms of interpretation and sensemaking (Stacey, 2000). Boundary objects (e.g. drawings, reports, models, prototypes, etc.) are best suited to serve as repositories for large amounts of codified explicit information. Despite the fact that most project teams use upwards of 50 different types of boundary objects, the majority of information on construction projects is still tacit (i.e. 83% according to Hanlon and Sanvido, 1995). With the interaction of all these different people and objects, there is a significant risk of small inefficiencies or conflicts compounding and negatively affecting information flow. Therefore, understanding the social and technical characteristics of both people and boundary objects ends up being critical in understanding their role in information flow.

People
There are two sets of characteristics that influence a person's role in information flow. The first set is based on their technical characteristics (i.e. the knowledge that an individual *actually* possesses). These characteristics are influenced by:

- Formal training (e.g. schooling, certifications)
- Informal training (e.g. independent research, second-hand knowledge gained through discussions with others)
- Experiential knowledge (e.g. first-hand knowledge gained from practice)
- Ability to apply one's knowledge to novel situations

The second set of characteristics is based on their social characteristics (i.e. how knowledgeable a person is *perceived to be* by others). These depend on an individual's:

- Status
- Personality
- Contractual role

Status, or position, can be evaluated in terms of an individual's position within their parent organization or position within the project team. The ubiquitous business card helps to clearly spell out the status of an individual (e.g. senior project manager, Ph.D., senior vice president, director of marketing, etc.). These all create an expectation and perception of the type of information and the quality of information that that individuals should be able to provide. I've seen many situations where junior engineers provide technically sound information to a team that goes unnoticed, and then the principal at same firm comes to the next meeting and says exactly the same thing, except that now everyone is furiously scribbling it down. Titles often matter most in initial interactions or in teams that meet very infrequently. Over time, teams will gain a true understanding of the types and quality of information that an individual can provide and that will override the letters on their business cards.

Personality is more complicated and multi-faceted than status. There is an entire field of organizational behavior research that deals with understanding personality and its effects on performance. Among the many traits that researchers have studied, the following have been dubbed the "Big Five":

- Extraversion is the predisposition to experiencing positive emotional states and feeling good about oneself and the world. It has a strong influence on performance when the job involves interacting with others, specifically when it is necessary to influence others (Barrick et al, 2001).
- Emotional Stability is the tendency toward neuroticism or feeling distressed. It has an influence on the quality of work and the ability to interact with others.
- Agreeableness is the ability to get along well with others. It is important when tasks involve helping and cooperating with others.
- Conscientiousness is the extent to which an individual is careful, pays attention to detail, and is self-disciplined.
- Openness to experience is the extent to which an individual is original, has broad interests, and is willing to take risks. This is strongly related to creativity and the ability to adapt to change (George & Zhou, 2001).

These traits influence an individual's likeability, perceived trustworthiness, and perceived quality of information. While an individual's personality can give an indication of how the individual will perform, in collaborative environments the interaction of differing personalities and the social dynamic that results is just as important. This will be discussed in greater detail in subsequent chapters.

Contractual role is included as a social characteristic because it creates *an expectation* in the minds of others about the information that an individual should be providing. Where a person's technical characteristics align with their contractual role, there is usually very little trouble. However, when an individual lacks the technical characteristics to support their contractual role, there is often a problem since they don't have the technical competencies to fulfill their role and support the team. Similarly, when an individual's technical expertise overlaps with the scopes covered by the contractual roles of others, there is potential for conflict. Whether this conflict is constructive or destructive often depends on the personality traits of the individuals involved. For example, on one project there was a consultant whose contractual role was to identify and resolve performance-related issues with the exterior wall design. However, because he had 10+ years experience as a contractor, he was asking the contractors some very detailed questions about the means and methods they intended to use. Because of the consultant's personality, the contractors interpreted his questions as threatening and complained that "he's being too nit-picky... we're the contractor...that's why they hired us... to figure this stuff out" and subsequently were more protective with the information that they shared in the future.

Boundary Objects
Boundary objects constitute the other main type of information source/receiver. In the information sciences, the term "boundary object" is used to describe an information artifact that spans two or more groups and thereby serves as a mechanism to transfer information across organizational, spatial, or temporal boundaries from one group to another

(Star, 1989). In the case of construction projects there can be upwards of 50 to 75 different types of boundary objects. These range from reports, project drawings, shop drawings, product submittals, requests for information, change order forms, schedules, building information models, code approvals, meeting minutes, etc. Each of these objects serves a specific purpose and is used to transfer information between parties or between phases. Similar to the people involved with a project, boundary objects also have their own technical and social characteristics that influence their role in information flow.

Boundary objects, by their nature, are capable only of capturing explicit information. However, they have different technical characteristics that influence the types of information that they can capture and subsequently disseminate back to the team in future interactions. The main technical characteristics loosely parallel those of the information itself. They are: 1) "richness" or the number of dimensions that the object is capable of capturing, 2) the technical scopes or content types that the object is intended for, and 3) the level of abstractness that the object is intended to capture.

Regarding richness, there are countless dimensions of information that could be captured by objects. For example, in the design of a building, most of the focus is on the three spatial dimensions and the relative orientation of different parts of the design. However, the project team also needs to consider the dimensions of time, cost, and contractual responsibility. Throughout the entire design and construction process, there are other dimensions of information that can be helpful, such as narratives about the history of a decision, alternate options, performance requirements, etc. Objects that can capture more dimensions provide more detailed information and more accurately capture the collective knowledge of the team. Interactions that revolve around these "richer" objects also result in more substantive discussions because there is less ambiguity due to individual interpretation. The challenge is that richer objects tend to be more complex and often require additional administrative work, specific expertise in managing the object, additional cost, or specialized equipment and training to utilize them (e.g. immersive building information modeling).

Boundary objects can be designed to capture specific scopes of information. Since certain boundary objects are typically used during particular phases or introduced by particular team members, they tend to be geared toward the types of information that are important to those individuals at that particular time. For example, objects used during construction, such as schedules, budgets, and logistics plans, are structured to emphasize constructability-related information (e.g. cost, sequencing of work, and means and methods). The same is true for other boundary objects designed to capture information related to design or performance (e.g. drawing sets and consultant field reports). In cases where boundary objects play a central role in a project, the information that they are designed to capture can actually dictate the overall focus and the processes of the team. As a result, each phase of project delivery tends to have its own set of boundary objects that have been developed and refined to address the needs of that phase and the players involved during that phase. However, because each phase tends to have its own objects, there are often additional processes, team members, and objects needed to help translate that information from the boundary objects of one phase to those of subsequent phases.

Boundary objects are also capable of capturing certain levels of abstractness. Specifically, there are objects that can capture: 1) intent; 2) process description; 3) product description; and 4) conformance. Intent objects capture and disseminate the goals and abstract properties of a certain aspect of the project (e.g. basis of design documents and qualitative user group studies). Process description objects, such as action plans, describe specific tasks and workflows, the roles and responsibilities of those involved, and how the work of those individuals will be coordinated. Product description objects, such as drawings, provide information regarding the technical characteristics or various components, their relationships to one another, and their relationship to the overall project. Finally, conformance objects provide information regarding whether the product description met the intent or whether the as-built condition conforms to the product descriptions (e.g. design review comments, site visit reports, and testing reports). The most effectively integrated scopes of information are ones that have all four types of objects.

While structure and technical characteristics affect the type of information a boundary object can capture, there are other characteristics that are more "social" in nature. These social characteristics influence the *perceived importance* of the object and the information contained within it. Perceived importance is crucial because it influences not only the value of the information already captured in an object, but also the willingness of others to add new information to the object or use the information already captured within the object. Similar to the way that a person's status and personality can influence their perceived importance, boundary objects also have factors affecting their perceived importance. The three major social characteristics are: 1) control, 2) connectedness, and 3) familiarity.

In the absence of clear and tangible project goals, boundary objects have the tendency to default goals and therefore control the focus of project team efforts. For example, the format of meeting minutes acts as a guide for what should be discussed in a meeting. Similarly, in order to put together a set of drawings, the format of the drawings provides a guide for what information is important (e.g. there are specific portions of the drawing set reserved for floor plans, elevations, and details). While the format of boundary objects can define information needs (i.e. the questions that the project team needs to provide information for), it also defines the explicit information that is readily available to the team to address future questions. In both of these cases, the entity responsible for developing the format of the objects, capturing the information, and maintaining the object can have a subtle, but significant, influence over the focus and collective memory of the project team.

Another determinant of perceived importance is the boundary object's link to other objects. The relationship that an object has to other objects within the project becomes a significant indication of that object's perceived importance. For example, stand-alone objects tend to only enjoy limited importance. However, objects that are tied to other objects end up compounding their importance because of their association. Specifically, there are three relationships that object can have with other objects (see Figure 3):
- Nested objects, i.e. where the information in one objects becomes a subset of the information in an overarching object;
- Coupled objects, i.e. where two objects are capturing very similar information but are created by different entities;
- Linked objects, i.e. where one object informs several others (essentially the inverse of the nested relationship).

Coupled objects commonly occur at transitions between phases or shifts in power to make sure that the important information is understood by both entities. One important type of linked relationship is when an object is explicitly linked to contractual obligation or some other means of justifying payment. Not surprisingly, these types of objects tend to hold greater perceived importance.

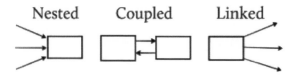

Figure 3: Types of Links Between Boundary Objects

Finally, there is the matter of familiarity; quite simply, objects that people know and are comfortable with tend to have greater importance. Objects that have been commonly used on past projects tend to enjoy, at least initially, a higher level of trust and importance. However, if new objects are introduced and demonstrate their value quickly, their importance increases.   In addition, if an individual has a role in developing an object, then their familiarity and commitment to using that object also increases. There are three basic means of developing and capturing information for boundary objects: they can be created individually; cooperatively, and collaboratively. Individually-constructed boundary objects are created by a single entity and although they may have high importance to those who created it, they also require buy-in from any others that will be using the information in the object. Cooperatively-constructed boundary objects are ones that are subdivided and different entities are responsible for select components of the objects (essentially a nested relationship).   Although each contributor has some accountability toward the cooperative object in its entirety, they still are primarily concerned with (and committed to) their portion. Collaborative-created boundary objects are also created collectively by different entities, but in such a way that each entity's contributions are inseparable from the others. In the case of collaborative objects, there is no choice but to have collective buy-in and accountability for the quality of the information captured in the object. In the case of collaborative objects, there is no choice but to have collective buy-in and accountability for the quality of the information captured in the object.

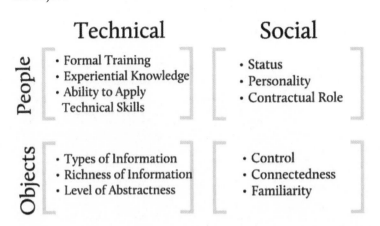

Figure 4: Socio-Technical Characteristics of People and Objects

Together, these social and technical characteristics influence the role and effectiveness that people and objects play in information flow (see Figure 4). However, it is important to note that none of these characteristics can be considered in isolation. Information flow is just as social as it is technical and therefore requires an awareness of both.

The Path: Interactions
Understanding the characteristics of people and objects is important. However, information flow cannot actually occur until these components are brought together in some sort of interaction. People commonly make the mistake of thinking that by simply bringing several components together, information will automatically flow. Interactions only create an *opportunity* for information flow; the effectiveness of an interaction is dependent on the combination of the people and objects involved and a number of interactional factors.

Ultimately, these interactional factors determine whether information will get incorporated into a project.

Figure 5 shows the typical inputs and outputs that occur within the interactions of a project team. There are two main types of information inputs: old and new. Old information inputs include: 1) parameters that have been set by past decisions, 2) the collective memory of the group regarding past interactions, and 3) information that can be retrieved from boundary objects. New information includes information related to questions raised in previous interactions (expected new information) and spontaneous contributions of new information (unexpected new information).

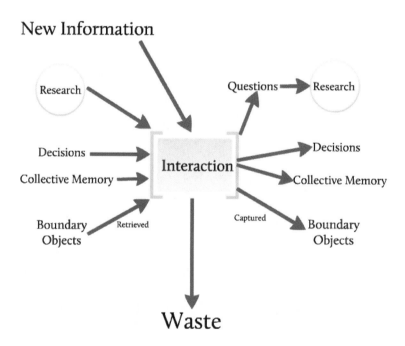

Figure 5: Interaction Inputs and Outputs

Of the new information made available during an interaction, some of it results in additional questions that drive future information needs, some results in decisions, some serves to modify the collective memory of the project team, and some gets captured in boundary objects. Although questions, collective memory, and boundary objects keep the information "alive" and available to the project team, the information does not really add value until it gets incorporated into the project by resulting in some sort of decision.

Unfortunately, there is also a significant amount of information that never gets captured by any of these means and results in information waste. There are several ways in which new information can become waste. With interpersonal interactions (i.e. between individuals), information provided by an individual can be accepted, rejected, or ignored (see Figure 6).

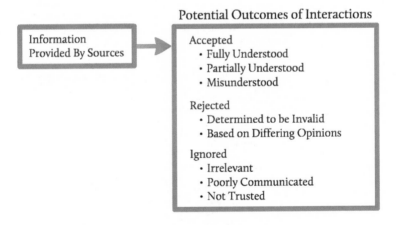

Figure 6: Potential Outcomes in Interpersonal Interactions

Ideally, valuable information is accepted. However, even if information is accepted, it can be fully understood, partially understood, or misunderstood. In some cases of partial understanding or misunderstanding, the receivers are aware of their incomplete understanding and can ask for clarification or additional information. If unaware, then the incomplete or incorrect understanding often results in lost information (i.e. waste) and occasionally conflict. Alternatively, information can also be rejected or ignored if the receiver did not perceive the value of the information being shared by the source. Rejected information is the result of a conscious determination that the information is not valid based on differences of opinion or perceived untruth. For example, when asked about something the superintendent had brought up during the meeting, the owner's representative dismissed it and added: *"With all due respect, he has no idea what he is talking about"*. Ignoring, on the other hand, is a less conscious process where information lacks perceived value and therefore is forgotten almost immediately after it was shared. When asking individuals about information that seemed to be ignored during the interaction, they often did not remember it being shared or commented that they did not really understand why the person had shared the information in the first place.

Similarly, there are certain outcomes that result from people-object interactions. In the use of boundary objects, there are two complementary types of interactions that take place: Person-to-object interactions (i.e. capture of information) and object-to-person interactions (i.e. retrieval of information). As depicted in Figure 7, boundary objects act as a mediator of information between two individuals or groups. However, because of the object's structure, information often has to be modified so that it can be captured in an object (e.g. summarized or paraphrased to fit the object's format). This often makes the information available for future retrieval different from what was originally provided by the source. This two-part transfer of information introduces two opportunities for information loss or misinterpretation. However, any information that is accurately captured remains available for the duration of the project and is less likely to be lost or skewed based on the fading recollections of individuals.

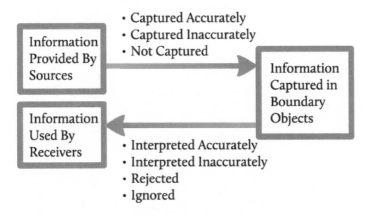

Figure 7: Potential Outcomes in Person-Object Interactions

With object-related interactions, there is also a spectrum of outcomes for information. In the person-to-object interactions (i.e. information capture), information could be: 1) captured accurately, 2) captured inaccurately or inadequately, or 3) not captured. These outcomes are mainly governed by the technical characteristics of the object and the technical characteristics of the person managing the boundary object. Information that was not captured becomes unavailable to future users of that boundary object unless it is reintroduced by another means, while information that is captured (whether accurately or inaccurately) is available for use in future interactions.

Object-to-person interactions (i.e. information retrieval) are similar to interpersonal interactions; the information available in the object can be interpreted accurately, interpreted inaccurately, ignored, or rejected. An interesting note is that there are rarely objects that capture information accurately enough that they do not require additional information from the people involved with the initial information capture. For example, often a report, detail sketch, or change order needs some sort of additional explanation from individuals who generated the object.

Driving Force: Perceived Mutual Relevance
The last component needed for flow is a driving force. In the case of information flow, the driving force is a sense of mutual relevance between a source and a receiver (i.e. alignment between *available information* and *information needs*). This mutual relevance can be either cognitive-based (i.e. based on common understanding) or value-based (i.e. based on common goals or values).

From an energetic standpoint, perceived mutual relevance can manifest itself in one of two ways, either: 1) there is an information need that requires or "pulls" information from the sources of the corresponding knowledge (e.g. a question that needs an answer), or 2) there is unsolicited information that is shared and its presence triggers or "pushes" a need for it (e.g. an answer looking for a question). In most cases, pulling information results in substantially better information flow, because the information provided fits a known need so the chances are greater that the information will be valued and understood. Pushing information is riskier because it relies on the receiver's ability to understand the information's relevance and apply it to the right issue.

In teams where individuals have worked together for long periods of time or where members come from similar functional backgrounds (e.g. within a single firm), there is a level of implied mutual relevance that has already been developed through past interactions. However in shorter-term collaborations or situations where individuals come from vastly different functional perspectives (e.g. project teams), mutual relevance needs to be developed. The sooner and more effectively that both cognitive and value-based mutual relevance can be developed within a team, the more effective their information flow and value creation will be. The key is understanding what is needed to establish common values and common understanding.

In talking with individuals about what influences the effectiveness of information flow, there are certain words that repeatedly come up: accountability, ambiguity, commitment, competence, conflict potential, context, intensity, relevance, respect, risk-taking, transparency, trust, etc. All of these factors have cognitive and emotional components to them, but at their most basic level come down to four major moderators: trust, commitment, learning, and understanding. Chapter two discusses each of these major moderators in greater detail and chapter three links them into a model that explains the pivotal role they collectively play in moderating information flow effectiveness.

Chapter 2

Trust, Commitment, Learning, and Understanding

Each of us has our own notions of what is meant by "trust", "commitment", "learning", and "understanding". However, since these concepts are so vital to information flow, they warrant some in-depth discussion. There are individuals who have dedicated their lives to furthering our understanding of these concepts. This chapter only skims the surface of this fascinating work. The intent is to provide a working knowledge of these constructs so that we can appreciate their complexity and begin to understand their critical role as information flow moderators.

Trust

Trust can be defined as "a psychological state comprising positive expectations about the behavior or intentions of another party, when one is vulnerable to that party" (Rousseau et al., 1998: p. 395). This definition essentially frames trust as the product of three important components: 1) it is a psychological state (i.e. influenced by both rational and emotional judgments), 2) it is comprised of expectations (e.g. based on some past experience, we think that we know how others will behave), and 3) we are vulnerable to the outcome of another's behavior (i.e. it matters to us).

Another means of understanding trust is to look at it in terms of social exchange theory. Social exchange theory states that relationships are developed through a series of voluntary actions where individuals are motivated by expected returns on their actions. As long as there is perceived mutual benefit then the exchanges continue, but if there is no perceived benefit to one party, then the exchanges taper off. While social exchange theory paints a fairly opportunistic view of trust, it should be noted that "benefit" can encompass several factors including learning (work-related or non-work related), feeling a sense of belonging, establishing a good reputation, establishing friendship, or feeling a sense of personal satisfaction.

A major component of trust is expectation. How do we develop expectations about individuals and situations with whom or which we have no prior history with? Initially, there is a phenomenon called "swift trust" that is based on similarities (e.g. similar backgrounds, experiences, or even of similar demographic characteristics such as age or nationality). These similarities create an initial sense of trust because they *suggest* similar goals and values (Kramer, Brewer, & Hanna 1996). However, the opposite is also true; often there is residual distrust of individuals or situations that share common characteristics of negative past experiences. For example, a colleague of mine had a stressful interaction with a German architect on one project. Sometime later, on a different project, he had to work with an Austrian architect and was preparing for the worst simply based on the similarities in accent. However, as he and the Austrian architect had more interactions, the initial "swift distrust" gave way to a more neutral and eventually positive relationship. Swift trust (or distrust) simply determines the starting point for an interaction and quickly gives way to trust based on the actual behaviors of that individual. There are certain ways that managers and leaders can improve trust among their team. Folger and Bies (1989) outlined seven key characteristics (truthfulness, justification, respect, feedback, consideration of others' views, consistency, and bias suppression) that are needed to create a sense of trust and fairness between individuals.

There are two main types of trust: 1) cognitive trust based on the reliability, integrity, or fairness of the other party or 2) affective trust based on care and concern about another's welfare. For example, on one project I was monitoring the work of a waterproofing subcontractor. As might be expected, there was very little initial trust between the watchful consultant and the contractors being watched. They were concerned that I might notice something that they were doing wrong and expose them, so they covered up questionable areas and worked differently when I was nearby. However, instead of just standing over them watching their every move, I took the opportunity to better understand their perspective on the work that they were doing (i.e. how they felt about the various details that we had designed, whether there were any problem areas they could foresee, and how they might prefer to detail certain aspects of the system). By soliciting their input, I was able to gain insight regarding their perspective and learn about the physical and psychological issues related to constructability of my design. At the same time, by my taking a genuine interest in their thoughts and opinions, the contractors felt valued and empowered to think about their work, explain their thoughts, and be more conscientious about what they were doing. These initial interactions served as a basis for establishing cognitive trust. However, as these interactions carried on, some of the conversations became more personal as we learned about each other's hometowns, families, hobbies, horses, favorites foods, etc. In these later interactions, both the subcontractors and I continued to benefit from the interactions as we learned interesting aspects of non-work related topics. However the interactions also allowed the trust to shift from cognitive trust to more of an affective trust and greatly increased our willingness to engage in very open and candid discussions about contentious work issues and resolve difficult issues amicably.

This example illustrates some interesting aspects of trust related to risk-taking that have also been observed in controlled research studies. Studies have shown that trust facilitates the willingness to take a risk in a relationship. Specifically regarding information flow, risk-taking can manifest itself in cooperative behavior, sharing sensitive information, bringing up a controversial idea, or investing additional resources to help accomplish a common goal. Trust is necessary for individuals if they are going to take a chance in offering their unique opinions and ideas or if they are going to be forthright about their lack of knowledge about a topic. If trust is not present, then others may call into question the underlying motive for offering an idea and not realize the inherent value of those ideas. There are also cyclical relationships that happen regarding trust and information sharing. In high trust relationships, parties take risks with each other and trust levels are enhanced. In low trust relationships, information is withheld that then leads to less acceptance of responsibility, more conflict, more questioning of others' motivations, and as a result, lower levels of trust.

Trust also impacts how another party and their actions are perceived (retrospectively) because it influences how individuals interpret current actions based on what has happened in the past (Dirks & Ferrin, 2001). For example, Robinson (1996) found that employees with low trust tended to interpret a breach of contract as intentional and negative, whereas employees with high trust tended to interpret it as unintentional or as a misunderstanding.

Trust also plays an interesting role in the perception of conflict. Substantive conflict provides the necessary "raw materials" for better task outcomes by fueling insightful discussions and bringing up important questions. However, trust moderates the extent that substantive conflict translates into affective conflict (i.e. people taking it personally). For example, I was attending a project team meeting regarding a problematic interface detail between a glass railing and a plaza deck waterproofing system. Prior to the meeting, I was talking with the architect and he had made a comment that generated some good discussion. This conversation resulted in some potential solutions for the detail in question. He made the same comment during the meeting, and the railing contractor (who had not been part of the earlier conversation) jumped down his throat and went on a 10-minute tirade complete with personal attacks. It was exactly the same comment – neutrally delivered – but the presence or absence of trust made all the difference in the type of discussion that followed.

Commitment

Commitment, in the context of this book, refers specifically to an individual's commitment to a particular organization. In the construction industry, the organizations in question are the parent firm of the individual and the temporary organization made up of the multi-disciplinary project team. Porter et al. (1974) define organizational commitment as the relative strength of an individual's identification with and involvement in a particular organization. This identification can be characterized by: 1) a strong belief in and acceptance of the organization's goals and values; 2) a willingness to exert considerable effort on behalf of the organization; and 3) a strong desire to maintain membership in the organization (Porter et al, 1974). Commitment is important to both the individual and the organization because it has a significant effect on job satisfaction and individual performance (Koch and Steers 1976, Mowday et. al. 1974).

Understanding "identity" is a precursor to understanding the development of organizational commitment. According to social identity theory, an individual's self-image is made up of a composite of their personal identity and their social identity (Tajfel and Turner 1986). Personal identity is a function of an individual's physical attributes, interests, values, abilities, and psychological traits. Social identity is based on an individual's perception of belonging to a specific group (Ashford and Mael 2004). These social classifications (i.e. the social categories into which individuals classify themselves) allow individuals to cognitively order their social environment; for example, people from work, friends, family, activity partners, community, etc. (Goode 1960). As individuals go from simply identifying with a given group in name only to a point where they have internalized the group's attitudes and values, they develop more of an overlap between a social identity and a personal identity.

While identity and commitment are similar and closely related constructs, they differ in terms of their essential meaning (Meyer et. al., 2006). An individual's identities are the objects for commitment, but it is the level (or intensity) of commitment given to each identity that creates an individual's salience hierarchy (i.e. how they really view themselves). Thoits (1983) found that individuals with many identities (i.e. integrated individuals) have relatively less commitment for each as opposed to individuals who only have a few identities (i.e. isolated individuals). For this reason, increased commitment toward one identity tends to decrease commitment toward others unless the various roles are somehow linked.

Ellemers and Rink (2005) identified two configurations for linking identities: 1) nested identities and 2) cross-cutting (i.e. overlapping) identities. Nested identities entail situations where in order for an individual to be a member of one organization, they have to be a member of another organization (e.g. such as working within a subgroup within a larger organization). Nested identities create a reinforcing effect for both since the one is a subset of the other. Cross-cutting or overlapping identities allow one aspect of an individual's identity to serve multiple organizations (e.g. an engineer who works for a structural design firm and is also a member of the American Society of Civil Engineers).

Although overlapping identities certainly reinforce a particular aspect of an individual's identity, they could reinforce or dilute an individual's commitment to either organization depending on the compatibility of goals, values, and norms (Hernes 1997).

In addition to identity theory, there has been some great research in understanding the different types of commitment. In 1991, Meyer and Allen compiled much of the commitment research to date in order to form the basis for their descriptions of the three types of commitment: affective commitment; continuance commitment; and normative commitment. They describe the three types of commitment as different psychological states, specifically:

> *Affective commitment refers to the employee's emotional attachment to, identification with, and involvement in the organization. Employees with a strong affective commitment continue employment with the organization because they want to do so. Continuance commitment refers to an awareness of the costs associated with leaving the organization. Employees whose primary link to the organization is based on continuance commitment remain because they need to do so. Finally, normative commitment reflects a feeling of obligation to continue employment. Employees with a high level of normative commitment feel that they ought to remain with the organization. (Meyer and Allen 1991)*

In this meta-analysis of commitment literature, Meyer and Allen (1991) found that personal characteristics, job characteristics, and work experiences are the major influences on commitment. Meyer et al (2002) found that all types of commitment are affected by personal characteristics (e.g. age, tenure, sex, and education). Affective commitment is influenced by work experiences, especially those that make the employee feel psychologically comfortable (e.g. approachable managers, equitable treatment) and highly competent (e.g.

challenging tasks and feedback) (Allen and Meyer 1996). Since continuance commitment develops from the employee's recognition of their investments into the company (e.g. time, effort, and pension contributions), it is influenced by availability of comparable alternatives. Normative commitment is influenced by how integral an individual feels to the organization, but may also be strongly influenced by cultural- or family-based values (Allen and Meyer 1996).

There are important process issues that influence the type of commitment. O'Reilly and Chatman (1986) found that the two major mechanisms that influence affective commitment are identification and internalization. Identification is based on exchange, where a member's desire to remain in an organization and their willingness to exert effort is due to the benefits that they receive from their relationship with the organization. Internalization has to do with shared values between an individual and the organization and is related to other issues of person-organization fit. Continuance commitment is subject to any process that increases the cost of leaving. Major contributors to continuance commitment include side bets, investments, and perceived non-transferability of skills and education (Meyer et al 2002). Normative commitment is heavily influenced by the internalization of cultural, familial, and organizational socialization experiences (Davis and Luthans, 1980). In addition, normative commitment is affected by internalized reciprocity mechanisms that cause members to feel obligated to support an organization based on special favors or investments that the organization has made to that member (Eisenberger et. al., 1986).

Having strongly committed individuals is critical to the success of organization. Optimally, it is best to have affectively committed members, i.e. individuals who feel passionate about the work that they are doing. Affectively committed individuals have higher performance, stronger intentions to remain, lower stress levels, and exhibit more organizational citizenship behaviors (e.g. go above and beyond their formal job descriptions). However, there is a spectrum of commitment levels that stretches from strong affective commitment at one end to an individual's decision to leave an organization at the other end. In a negative downward spiral, an individual's strong affective commitment can first weaken into moral obligation (i.e. normative commitment coupled with weak affective commitment), then indebted commitment (i.e. normative commitment coupled with continuance commitment), then pure continuance commitment, and finally no commitment (i.e. leaving the organization). In a positive upward spiral, individuals join an organization because there is no better option and their initial commitment is based on their gratitude for being given a job (indebted commitment). As they continue to work there, they start to care about the individuals they are working with and the role that they play within the organization. As a result, their indebted commitment becomes more of a moral commitment. If the organization's goals are closely aligned with the individuals' and they become passionate about their work, then their commitment finally morphs into strong affective commitment.

One critical question for organizations is how they can increase their members' commitment toward the organizations. Based on social identity theory, one means of accomplishing this is for organizations to find ways to nest or overlap organizational commitment with their members' other commitments (e.g. by providing support for family, other professional activities, personal interests, etc.) so that their organizational commitment piggybacks on their other personal commitments. However, there is only so much that an organization can nest or overlap with its members' other commitments and still keep a strong focus on its own organizational goals.

To explore other means of increasing commitment, it is necessary to understand that each commitment type encompasses different psychological states. Continuance commitment is fundamentally an economic evaluation of the pros and cons for various options. Normative commitment is based on an individual's association with a group of people. Affective commitment is based on an individual's being able to pursue and fulfill personal goals and passions. Therefore, there are several psychological mechanisms by which individual commitment to an organization can change. When looking at decreasing commitment, the primary cause for a shift from affective commitment to normative commitment seems to be disappointment or disenchantment on the part of the individual regarding the alignment between the organization's values and the individual's personal values. Affectively committed individuals believe that the organization shares their own personal values. If their actual experiences differ from their expectations, that difference triggers disappointment. These differences can be triggered by violations of implicit relational contracts between the organization and the individual (e.g. low work challenge level, lack of opportunities for advancement or professional growth, disappointment with the organization in terms of dependability or support, ambiguous roles and conflict, abusive leadership, and inequitable treatment). Violation of these psychological contracts creates an emotional response that negatively affects motivation and commitment levels of individuals in an organization (Rousseau, 1995). Inequity, for example, or even the perception of inequity, has been shown to negatively affect trust in the organization as well as organization commitment.

Even if individuals become disappointed with the formal organization, they can still have strong, positive commitment toward constructs related to the organization such as subgroups or the importance of their work to society. This normative commitment stems from individuals' perceived obligation toward peers and subordinates, to their cultural, familial, or individual norms, or to the greater good. Although this commitment is only indirectly applicable to the formal organization, it still creates a moral obligation between members and the organization. However, if members reach a point where they no longer understand or see the value in their role as part of the organization, then their normative commitment has no grounding (i.e. they no longer feel as an integral part of the group). Severe or frequent abuses or disappointments that create stress or disassociation, a lack of purpose or role clarity for the individual, or negative socialization experiences with peers, superiors, or subordinates can trigger disassociation and, in turn, lead to an individual deciding to leave the organization.

Regarding increases in commitment, the converse is true; mechanisms such as association and inspiration allow individuals to develop more beneficial types of organizational commitment to an organization. In order for individuals who have primarily continuance commitments to develop more of a normative commitment, they need to feel as though they are a valued part of the organization. This can happen through providing transparency in organizational structure and policy so that individuals realize their value to the organization. It can also be accomplished by investing in the individual (e.g. training or continuing education) or the formation of work groups to help increase an individual's sense of importance and connection to others in the organization. All of these measures, in addition to praise and other extrinsic rewards, can gradually increase the association between individuals and an organization. With increased association, continuance commitment gives way to social and moral obligation and opens the door to opportunities for affective commitment.

However, moving from normative commitment to affective commitment requires more than simply creating an association between individuals and the organization. To foster affective commitment, individuals need to become intrinsically motivated and inspired to contribute to the mission of the organization. By empowering individuals through giving them autonomy, creation of self-managing teams, or challenging them to expand their potential, organizations help individuals become much more personally involved with their success and consequently the success of the organization. This personal involvement allows them to align their own personal characteristics with their roles in the organization. Figure 8 illustrates the psychological mechanisms that can trigger changes in commitment level.

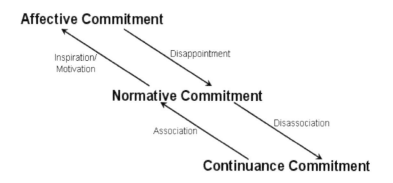

Figure 8: Triggers for Changes in Commitment Level

Learning
Learning is generally thought of as the acquisition of knowledge or information (Saljo, 1979). However, once information is acquired, it can be utilized in different ways. One use for learned information is that it can simply be recalled (e.g. memorization of facts, repetitive processes, mechanistic application of skills). Learned information can also be used for sensemaking and abstracting meaning to interpret a given situation. This is known as single-loop

learning (i.e. new information that enriches an individual's existing knowledge base). Finally, new information can be used to understand reality in a different way (i.e. learning that results in a fundamental change in one's existing knowledge base). This process is known as double loop learning because it involves two feedback loops: one related to learning about the consequences of actions and another that relates to changing the underlying assumptions that make up an individual's knowledge base. While double-loop learning is much more profound and valuable to an individual, it requires a very rich flow of information and a psychologically safe environment.

In addition to thinking about the types of learning that can occur, it is also important to understanding the processes by which learning can occur. The four major perspectives related to the process of learning are the: 1) behaviorist orientation, 2) cognitive orientation, 3) humanistic orientation, and 4) the social/situational orientation (Smith, 1999). Each differs in how it characterizes learning, its perspective on the major triggers that enable learning, and the implications are for creating learning environments.

The behaviorist perspective views learning as something that causes a change in behavior. It considers learning as a result of environmental stimuli and not characteristics of the individual. The key drivers are contiguity (i.e. the proximity of two events in time) and reinforcement (i.e. anything that increases the likelihood of an event recurring) (Merriam and Caffarella, 1991: 126). With his work on operant conditioning, B.F. Skinner further developed this notion of rewarding behaviors that you want to recur and ignoring or punishing behaviors that are less undesired. This perspective has implications for how incentives or penalties are incorporated into interpersonal interactions.

Whereas individuals with a behaviorist orientation focus on the role of the environment in learning, those with a cognitive orientation seek to understand learning in terms of what happens in the individual's mind. Jean Piaget's work with child and adolescent development gave insight as to the mental processes that enable early learning. However, when these mental processes are applied to adult learning there are some key principles that emerge. The first is that instruction should be well organized and clearly structured. This allows individuals exposed to new information to more easily understand inferences, expectations, and connections (Hartley, 1998). The second principle is that different individuals focus on different aspects of the environment and therefore the way that information is presented plays a role in how different people understand it. Harvard psychologist Howard Gardner developed his theory of multiple intelligences (1983) stating that there are seven ways that individuals enhance their understanding of their world:

- *Linguistic* (ability to use spoken or written words)
- *Logical/Mathematical* (ability to use numbers and patterns and to reason using inductive and deductive thinking)
- *Visual/Spatial* (ability to mentally visualize objects in space)
- *Body/Kinesthetic* (ability to control the body and physical motion)
- *Musical/Rhythmic* (ability to understand rhythms, tones, and beats)
- *Interpersonal* (ability to communicate effectively with others and develop relationships)
- *Intrapersonal* (ability to understand one's own emotions and motivations).

Depending on an individual's level and type of intelligence, there will be certain representations of information that are better suited to enable them to learn. The third aspect of cognitivism that influences adult learning is the notion that prior knowledge is important, i.e. new knowledge needs to be able to fit into a person's existing knowledge base in order for it to be meaningful. Finally, cognitivists recognize the benefit of non-physical reinforcement, i.e. cognitive feedback such as sharing feedback about a person's successes or failures can also serves as valuable reinforcement.

The humanistic perspective takes yet another angle on learning and views it primarily in terms of its role in realization of human potential. The most notable work in this area is Abraham Maslow's hierarchy of needs. Although heavily debated, Maslow's hierarchy provides a useful context for understanding the range of human psychological needs. This hierarchy states that lower needs need to be satisfied before an individual can pursue higher level needs. From most fundamental to most advanced, the needs range from:

1) Psychological needs (those needed for survival)
2) Safety needs (personal and financial security, health and well-being, etc.)
3) Love and belonging (friendship, intimacy, and family)
4) Self-esteem needs (confidence, independence, status, prestige)
5) Self-actualization (i.e. realizing the fullness of one's potential).

Humanists argue that most intellectual pursuits are a form of self-actualization although the can also be linked to other stages. This notion has significant implications for the type of environment that needs to exist for learning to occur (i.e. psychologically safe, trusting, inclusive, and comfortable). This is especially true for higher-order learning. Fiol and Lyles (1985) found that learning, especially double-loop learning, cannot happen in environments that are too complex and dynamic because it is a sensitive process that requires a balance between change and constancy.

Finally, there is the social/situation perspective that focuses on the social environment. This perspective combines two similar perspectives: 1) social learning (that focuses on learning as a result of observing others); and 2) situational/situated learning that focuses on learning as a process of social participation. Social learning theory (Bandura, 1977) states that we can learn from observing the consequences of other people's actions and therefore do not need to solely rely on the outcomes of our own actions to inform our behavior. Therefore, individuals may develop expectations based on observing interactions between others. Situated learning (Lave and Wenger, 1991) comes from involvement in a community of practice, e.g. individuals join a community of practice and first learn from observing at the periphery until they become more competent, at which point they begin to move to the center of the community. One of the classic examples of this is the artisan guilds or today's trade unions. These systems create a structured framework where individuals start off helping out more experienced members as apprentices, they work on refining their own skills as journeymen, and finally excel and innovate in their field as master craftsmen. Situated learning has implications for the timing of involvement in teams because it suggests that there may need to be a "warm up" period where individuals are peripherally involved prior to expecting them to effectively play a key central role in the team.

Understanding

People are rationally bounded; i.e. they are only capable of understanding only a limited amount of information. To cope with bounded rationality, people need to filter the overload of information to which they are subjected in a situation. The model of strategic choice developed by Hambrick and Mason (1984) provides a useful context to understand this phenomenon (Figure 9). At any given moment, there is a tremendous amount of information available to each of us: the words on a page, the air temperature, the colors, sounds, and smells around us, not to mention our thoughts. However, in order to function efficiently, individuals need to ignore the unimportant information and focus on the information that is most relevant to the task at hand. The first way that people filter through the infinite amount of information available is with their values and existing mental model. Together these create their frame of reference that subconsciously allows them to be aware of what is most important. From that information, they further filter information based on what they consciously feel is important. The information that makes it through all those filters is what they use to interpret the situation and make decisions. Because of differing frames of reference, different individuals can be exposed to the same situation and information, yet derive different ideas about the best course of action.

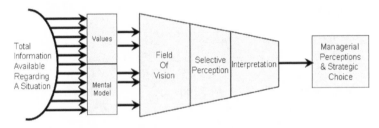

Figure 9: Model of Strategic Choice Under Conditions of Bounded Rationality (Hambrick and Mason, 1984). Here "mental model" was used in lieu of the original publication's "cognitive base".

For example, if there are two individuals in waiting in the reception area of a client's office to meet with someone, they will notice different things. One of the individuals may be more aesthetically inclined and currently in the process of renovating their home. She may notice the layout of the office, the paint color, the trim at the top of the wall, and especially

47

the way the furniture is laid out to subtly discourage people from walking in certain parts of the area. The other individual may be slightly neurotic about being on-time and may have a meeting immediately after this one and is not sure that he'll get there in time. This second individual is extremely aware of the clock on the wall, anyone walking down the hallway leading to the reception area, and every movement that the receptionist makes. These two individuals are in the exact same space at the exact same time and subject to the same information regarding the environment, yet their differing values and mental models give them completely different perspectives of their experience.

One of the major factors influencing the effectiveness of an interaction is how the various individuals interpret the same situation. Part of their interpretation comes from their cognitive understanding of the situation, while the other part comes from their values or feelings about the situation. In terms of their cognitive interpretations, it is necessary for individuals to continuously refine and adapt their understanding of a situation, especially in rapidly changing, information-intensive environments (Eisenhardt and Martin, 2000). Hambrick et. al. (2005) also observed that when demands are greater, situations require individuals to be more comprehensive in their understanding, yet cognitive limitations create the need to limit the amount of information and cognitive processes required of them. Therefore, the appropriateness of their filters becomes increasingly important.

One means of balancing comprehensiveness and cognitive limitations is through the use of schemas. Schemas, or mental models, can be programmed in individuals through training or developed organically through their cumulative experiences. Mental models provide the basis for understanding a situation and focusing our attention to the information that is critical to the task at hand. For example, when crossing the street, we are taught from an early age to look both ways for cars and cross at crosswalks (programmed mental model). However, if there was an occasion where an individual almost got hit by a person on a bicycle when crossing the street, then all of a sudden "looking for bicyclists" becomes a part of the street crossing mental model (organically developed from experience). As illustrated by this example, when an individual has a related experiences, her mental model become more abstract, complex, and organized (Fiske and Taylor, 1984).

In this book, the terms *mental model* and *schema* are used interchangeably, however most of the research in this area uses *schema* (from the Greek word for "shape "or "plan"). The literature focuses on four main types of schemas. The first is the *self schema* or an individual's notions about himself that are derived from past experience (e.g. what we like, dislike, or how we react to a given situation). The second type is the *person schema*, or how individuals categorize people. Fong and Markus (1982) found that people with a self-schema for a given attribute also specifically note that attribute in other people. The third type is a *script schema* that outlines the appropriate sequence of events in a given situation (Lord & Foti, 1986). The final type of schema is a compound *person-in-situation schema* that outlines the expectations of how an individual will behave in a situation.

These schemas allow individuals to reduce the amount of information that they need to process by simply plugging limited new information into their existing model to determine their course of action. The challenge in team environments is that it is necessary for different individuals (each with their own schemas) to agree to a common course of action. For this reason, team members need to learn from each other and develop a common understanding of a situation (i.e. complementary schemas) so that they can arrive at common solutions.

In order to modify their schemas (or mental models), individuals must go through a process of learning (Stacey, 1999: 169). In less complex environments, individuals can first engage in single-loop learning that applies new information from others to their existing mental model. In more complex environments, if there is also adequate psychological safety, they can also engage in double-loop learning where new information provided by the team fundamentally shifts each person's existing mental model resulting in greater alignment around the shared information.

Mental model convergence is essential in sharing and understanding information from others and critical to enabling group decision-making. Differing mental models often cause the transfer of information to be inefficient and prone to bias and distortion (Dearborn & Simon, 1958). These hazards only increase in environments with greater uncertainty (Lawrence & Lorsch, 1967; Tushman, 1977). So how do diverse teams in uncertain environments create enough common understanding to effectively communicate but not lose the value of differing perspectives? This particular dilemma is exactly why it is important to strike a balance between convergence and diversity of mental models. On the one hand, is the commonality that is needed for effective communication. On the other hand, expertise diversity is necessary in order to assure that the ideas are being evaluated critically. Chapter 4 will discuss the tensions between diversity and decision-making in greater detail.

Chapter 3

Trust and Learning Cycles

By studying team interactions, both positive and negative, we can begin to understand the phenomena that influence how we can most effectively get new information incorporated into a project. There is little question that the moderators of trust, commitment, learning, and understanding play a role in the performance of any project team or organization. However, when it comes to teams that need to process and integrate large amounts of new information (e.g. complex or innovative projects), these moderators become absolutely critical. In every situation, positive and negative outcomes can be explained by the presence or absence of trust, commitment, learning, and understanding. In fact, it is almost always a combination and never a single stand-alone moderator. Part of this is due to the cyclical nature of team interactions (i.e. past interactions influence the current dynamic and set the stage for future interactions). However, it also has to do with the fact that when it comes to information sharing, all four of those moderators are inextricably connected. They work together to influence how project teams seek information, share information, and accept information provided by others. These phenomena happen both at an emotional/psychological level and at a cognitive level.

At the emotional/psychological level, it's primarily the first two moderators, trust and commitment, that are of most interest. As was discussed in the previous chapter, trust involves having positive expectations about another's future actions when an individual is vulnerable to those actions.

Commitment is the strength of an individual's identification with and involvement in a particular organization and influences the willingness of that individual to exert effort toward common goals. Trust and commitment work together to shift a person's values regarding the project team with *trust being the reason* for the shift and increased *commitment being the outcome*.

Similarly, learning and understanding are the cognitive-focused moderators. Learning occurs when the processing of new information changes an individual's understanding and range of potential behaviors. Understanding is an internal process that occurs when individuals have internalized what they've learned and can adapt their knowledge to new and unique situations. Learning and understanding involve modification of a person's mental model (i.e. the basis for how individuals understand information). Similar to trust and commitment, *learning is the cause* and *understanding is the result* of this shift.

As these internal shifts occur in a collaborative team environment, they manifest themselves as shared commitment (through value convergence) and common understanding (through mental model convergence). These external manifestations are what are perceived by others and subsequently influence information sharing and information acceptance in future interactions. To put it another way, there are two simultaneous cycles that continuously shape and are shaped by the type of information shared and the way that it is shared. These two cycles are: 1) a trust/commitment cycle that is based on an individual's emotional valuation of the experience; and 2) a learning/understanding cycle that is based on an individual cognitive valuation of the information.

Valuation of the Experience:
The Trust/Commitment Cycle

The valuation of the experience depends on how an individual *feels* during an interaction. For example, in a given interaction, the participants are consciously and subconsciously aware of their perceptions of: 1) how others view them; 2) whether others value their information contributions; 3) the other team members' social and technical characteristics; 4) the value of the information shared by the other team members; 5) the social dynamic; and 6) their expectations for subsequent interactions.

Essentially, the types of information shared and the way the information is shared/received constantly modify how closely individuals identify with their role as a member of the project team. If their experiences result in higher levels of trust (i.e. positive expectations about others' willingness and ability to improve the situation), then there is a sense of shared values (i.e. convergence of values). This convergence not only strengthens the overlap between an individual's identity and their role in the project, but also increases their level of commitment to performing their role to help those who can in turn help them. It should be noted that an individual's "role" does not only refer to their technical role, but can also refer to their social role within the team. The level of commitment affects the quality and amount of information that an individual shares with the rest of the team in future interactions. It also affects the openness and willingness to understand information shared by others. These phenomena influence future information sharing behaviors and perpetuate additional iterations of the cycle (see Figure 10).

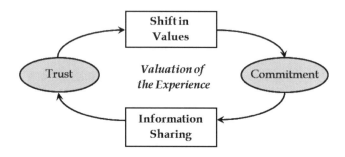

Figure 10:   Valuation of the Experience: The Trust/
Commitment Cycle

In positive iterations of this cycle, individuals feel that: 1) their
contributions are valued; 2) they are being treated fairly; 3)
they and others are being given responsibility but also held
accountable for those responsibilities (i.e. empowerment); 4)
their positive expectations are being met or exceeded; and 5)
other project team members share their commitment to team
goals. In these cases, individuals feel a greater identification
with the team and stronger commitment to the team outcome.
They are also more likely to contribute information, ask for
information from others, and engage in constructive debate.
In negative iterations, individuals feel the opposite and
therefore hold more tightly to their own values and remain
committed only to their individual goals. Subsequently, this
decreases the likelihood of individuals contributing new
information, paying attention or accepting information from
others, and their willingness to explain or entertain
constructive discussion.

Valuation of the Information:
The Learning/Understanding Cycle

Aside from the experience itself, a person's valuation of the actual information that is being shared also significantly affects information flow. If new information has enough of an overlap with an individual's existing mental model, then he can recognize the value of that information. Depending on how "valuable" specific information is to an individual, that individual may accept the information and learn from it, choose to reject, or subconsciously ignore it. There are several factors that influence which of these outcomes occur: 1) one's willingness to learn/openness to new ideas; 2) the clarity of the information; 3) the relevance of the shared information to one's existing mental model; and 4) an individual's trust of the person providing the information and the others present (i.e. psychological stability). When individuals engage in learning, they link new information to a part of their existing mental model that is most closely related to the new information (i.e. association). This process subsequently broadens or modifies their mental model (i.e. internalization). Depending on the significance of the new information, an individual may engage in either basic single-loop learning or higher-level double-loop learning (Stacey, 2000). When information shared by one team member enables another to learn, then their mental models begin to converge. As the mental models of various team members converge, individuals develop a greater awareness of how their knowledge relates to others and to the project in general (i.e. common understanding). This awareness results in team members sharing information that is more relevant to the needs of others and sharing in such a way that can be more easily understood by the intended receivers, thus perpetuating the cycle (see Figure 11).

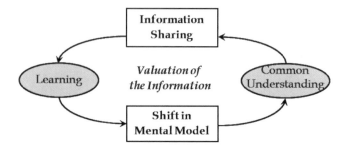

Figure 11: Valuation of the Information: The Learning/
Commitment Cycle

In positive iterations of this cycle, information is shared in a
way that is deemed valuable by others. Because of its greater
perceived value, it is more likely to be incorporated into their
mental model. It also may shift the way that an individual
understands and interprets information so that he is more
aligned with what others on the project team feel is valuable.
In subsequent interactions, individuals will share information
that they feel is relevant based on their common
understanding. Relevant information is more easily accepted,
facilitates learning, and results in further convergence of
mental models. In negative iterations, individuals do not
value or trust new information, so it is often ignored or
rejected and does not result in significant learning. As a result,
individuals retain their existing mental models and continue
to reiterate the same information as they did in past
interactions without understanding how to make it more
valuable to others. This often builds frustration among the
team members and decreases their willingness to share new
information or accept new information from others.

Interdependence of Trust and Learning

Although the trust/commitment cycle is predominantly responsible for convergence of values and the learning/understanding cycle for convergence of mental model, neither can happen in isolation from the other. In fact, they are intimately dependent upon each other. Trust and commitment can be strengthened only when: 1) others provide information that is helpful and supportive to an individual, or 2) when an individual feels that they are providing information that is valued by others. Both of these conditions can happen only through greater common understanding. Similarly, learning can occur only in psychologically safe environments where individuals trust the information provided by others and are committed enough to the project to engage in learning.

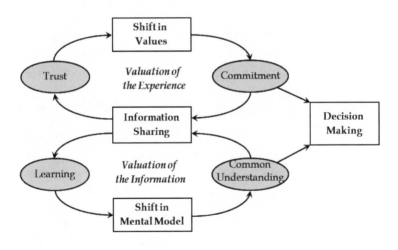

Figure 12: Interdependence of Trust and Learning Cycles

Because of these interdependencies, factors that affect one aspect of the interaction model influence all aspects. However, both of these cycles center on information sharing, specifically, the quality and relevance of information and the way in which the information is shared (see Figure 12). Information sharing is the most integral part of multi-disciplinary collaboration as it what allows diverse project teams to understand multi-faceted issues, conduct comprehensive analyses, and make informed decisions. The interconnected trust and learning cycles are the major determinants in whether relevant information accessible to the team will be firstly made available and secondly accepted by the project team. The two cycles are also the major influences regarding whether new information gets captured in decisions where it can truly add value to the project (this will be discussed further in Chapter 4).

Although most of the focus in this chapter is on interpersonal relationships, the same principles hold true for person-object interactions. The only difference is that boundary objects cannot adjust on their own, i.e. they rely on their administrator or manager to either modify their structure or the process of using them. Boundary objects demonstrate their value by helping project team members understand the project better or by providing a means to make the information contributions of the project team carry greater weight. Objects with greater perceived value command greater trust and commitment and that makes individuals more likely to contribute information to them, care about the quality of information captured within them, and use the information already captured within the object. Additionally, boundary objects that help individuals better understand aspects of the project can influence the structure of the team's mental models by the way that those objects organize information. For example, when a building is designed using two dimensional representations, designers convey the idea of the design by cutting slices through the building; wherever designers cut a slice through the building, they have to figure out the how all the components in that two dimensional view are organized. The problem is that there are conditions such as certain interfaces and transitions that are missed because the boundary object (i.e. the two dimensional drawing) does not explicitly show them. Developing a design in three dimensions, however, forces designers to focus on complex interfaces and transitions because the conflicts and interdependencies are clearly apparent to everyone using the object (i.e. the 3D model) and need to be figured out in order to "complete" the object. In this way, certain boundary objects can be valuable tools in enabling learning, development of common understanding, and developing trust through transparency and accountability.

Behaviors and Trends
Managers need to be aware of these moderators and their interrelation, but more importantly, they need to understand how to create positive iterations of these cycles within teams. While there is no singular means of influencing these cycles, there are several triggers that can be utilized to encourage positive iterations of trust and learning. In order to understand these triggers, we need to look at behavioral trends that occur within team interactions.

Information behaviors involve the ways that individuals seek information, share information, and respond to information from others. As individuals interact, certain subtle tendencies emerge surrounding these information-related activities. Often within the first few interactions, the behavioral cycles that will set the tone for all future interactions are already in play. Awareness of these subtle tendencies can provide project team managers with valuable insight and allow them to take more proactive measures to encourage positive information behaviors while mitigating negative ones.

Behaviors
Information behaviors are often difficult to understand, especially in situations where most of the information comes from fuzzy opinions and loose interpretations of past

experiences (as opposed to hard data from structured analyses). Information behaviors are very subtle and are often barely perceivable, but have a tremendous subconscious influence on the information flow within teams. Behaviors are so subtle that often individuals are not even aware of their own behaviors and the effect that they have on others. Part of the difficulty in developing an awareness of one's own behaviors is that it requires a significant amount of introspection (i.e. understanding why we feel the way we do and how those feelings manifest themselves in certain types of actions) which there is rarely time for on fast-paced complex projects. It also requires an objective perspective and realizing that people's actions are often projections of their own emotional state and therefore not always intentional.

For these reasons, in recent years there has been an increasing focus on emotional intelligence and emotional awareness. Several authors have researched and developed this notion of emotional intelligence and its effect on individual, team, and organizational performance. In my experience and observations of the behaviors prevalent in construction teams, there is one overarching factor that influences an individual's behavior: *self-confidence*. In different individuals, their level of self-confidence (and the corresponding insecurity) manifests themselves in different ways that link back to the four moderators of trust, commitment, learning, and understanding.

The first way that insecurity manifests itself is through avoidance (i.e. being unwilling to acknowledge one's own lack of understanding in an environment absent of trust). Avoidance stems from individuals feeling that they don't understand what is being discussed or asked of them, but also not feeling psychologically safe enough to ask for an explanation. There are behaviors that demonstrate passive avoidance such as giving ambiguous answers, not answering questions, or pretending to understand. There are also more active means of avoidance such as changing the topic of discussion, deflecting questions onto others, downplaying the importance of some issue, or simply giving misinformation and hoping that no one else knows any better. The converse types of behaviors, however, are demonstrated by individuals who are more secure and do not hesitate to ask questions, admit that they need to develop a better understanding, or take responsibility for finding answers or solutions to problems posed to them. While they are acknowledging their ignorance about the respective matter, they are also confident in their ability to figure it out and committed to helping the team fully understand various issues and find solutions.

The other way that insecurity manifests itself is through opportunism (i.e. trying to maintain a competitive advantage by keeping others on the team down). Opportunistic individuals are always seeking to improve their own position *relative* to others. Often, they fail to understand that in a team environment, their success is intimately dependent on the success of others. In some situations, there is the "knowledge is power" perspective, where an individual's position is advanced by withholding information or explanations that could help others better understand the project. In other situations, there are individuals who try to reduce others' standing within the team by constantly discrediting or assigning blame for issues rather than working toward a solution. There are also situations where individuals elevate their position by constantly pushing their individual goals and existing knowledge with the hope of getting the team goals to align with their personal goals (instead of the other way around). In non-opportunistic situations, individuals put the interests of the project, other team members, and themselves on an even level and realize that their success is intimately tied to the success of the other team members and the project.

The combinations of behaviors exhibited by the project team can result either in positive, mixed, or negative experiences for the team. Those experiences cause additional positive or negative iterations of trust and learning cycles that subsequently influence future information behaviors. In many cases, there are distinct trends and cycles that emerge as certain sets of behaviors occur concurrently.

Behavioral Cycles
Over the course of team interactions, three general trends emerge. The first trend involves sets of behaviors that gradually result in decreased information flow and deteriorating team performance (i.e. vicious cycles). The second trend involves sets of behaviors that result in continuous improvement of information flow and increased team effectiveness (i.e. virtuous cycles). The third involves a mix of behaviors that keep the interactions from getting substantially better or worse (i.e. aspects of both vicious and virtuous cycles that result in stable but only semi-efficient flow of information). Each of these trends has unique characteristics, qualitative descriptors, and outcomes.

Vicious Cycles
In general, teams that experience deteriorating information flow tend to have the following characteristics:
- Avoidance of complex issues (e.g. postponing decisions or providing overly ambiguous information that provides little basis for advancing the discussions);
- Reiteration of old information over and over again without adapting or elaborating upon it;
- Emphasis on the individual (e.g. pushing individual goals, self-preservation, defensiveness under questioning, and lack of interest in other team members' concerns).

These behaviors result in greater tensions and increasingly extreme behaviors during subsequent interactions. The following example illustrates some of these cycles:

A project team was working on the delivery of a high-profile cancer institute for a medical campus. In addition to the technical complexity of designing such a facility, it was also part of the new "face" of the campus so the architecture aesthetic was also important. There were several key architectural features of the exterior wall system that were central to the aesthetic intent of the building; however, even after the 75% construction drawing set had been released, several of these features were still missing critical information related to constructability and performance. The owner's representative (owner) was disappointed with the lack of useful information in the drawings and was also the kind of person who was not shy about making his opinion known. Since he had some significant design and construction experience, the owner conducted an informal internal review of the exterior wall design, created a spreadsheet of his comments, and pushed them in front of the soft-spoken architect and told him to address his concerns. At each meeting, the owner would ask the architect if he had addressed the concerns about the architectural features, to which the architect would give a reason why they had not. Gradually, the owner became even more adamant that they needed to address these issues and would push even harder for results (e.g. through more aggressive language, then he brought in an outside consultant to review the design, and eventually he added mock-up and in-situ performance testing requirements to make sure that the design would perform adequately). During this time, the architect only became more defensive and withdrawn in the project team interactions. The issues still remained unaddressed and because of the contentiousness of the issue, the architect began avoiding any conversations about the exterior wall systems. The owner's frustration spilled into conversations about other aspects of the project where he also began giving the architect a hard time. Finally, the owner brought on board the key subcontractors to assist the architect figure out the design. This only worsened the relationship between the owner and architect and the architect stopped attending meetings and sharing any non-essential information. Communication between the owner and architect essentially came to a halt and this tension began to negatively affect relationships among other project team members.

In this example, the interactions between the owner and architect created a vicious cycle of confrontation and avoidance. The overlap of the owner's architectural knowledge and the architect's knowledge created a condition for conflict. This had the potential to be a constructive interaction; however, the combination of the owner's intimidating personality, the complexity of the issues, and the soft-spoken architect's unwillingness to figure them out created a destructive situation. The architect could have taken the opportunity to ask for explanations regarding the issues that the owner was concerned with, or bring in her own consultant to help her understand the systems, but instead felt too threatened to exhibit anything that could be perceived as ignorance. For the owner's part, he felt that the architect was ignoring his concerns. The combination of distrust and avoidance (i.e. related to learning more about the issues) caused the owner to push even harder for his priorities and subsequently made the architect more defensive. Regarding information flow, this caused the architect to share even less information and caused the owner to keep reiterating the same old information and that only worsened the situation. They each became more extreme in their own differing perspectives and goals. This kept them from developing a common understanding and decreased their commitment to the project which only reinforced the vicious cycle.

Negative cycles are fed by certain recurring patterns of actions and reactions (i.e. a behavioral dyad, or pair of actions). The confrontation/avoidance dyad is one of the most prevalent instigators of negative cycles within project teams. Another common dyad is the confrontation/ misdirection cycle where individuals who are confronted with a challenging question dismiss the question by either providing an overly ambiguous answer or by talking about another topic that they could speak about more confidently. Another more subtle vicious cycle dyad is that of disrespect and withdrawal (i.e. the gradual withdrawal of individuals who either did not feel comfortable contributing information or whose prior information contributions were ignored).

The difficultly in working with information behaviors is that the clues and signals regarding what is really going on are often very subtle, so it requires careful observation of how people act and how they talk about their experience. When talking with individuals involved with these types of vicious cycles, their explanations referenced feelings related to:

- Insecurity, e.g. *"She needs to sound important, so if someone asks about something she doesn't know about, she just shifts the conversations to something that she does know about"*;
- Ignorance, e.g. *"They probably don't know what to do, so they are just hoping it will solve itself"*;
- Frustration and anger, e.g. *"If I hear that one more time, I might slap somebody - I want results!"*;
- Opportunism and risk aversity, e.g. *"We brought them in early to add value and instead they're just padding their bid"*;
- Lack of motivation, e.g. *"That doesn't walk the dog. It doesn't butter the biscuit. He needs to do whatever it takes to get them back here and figure this out."*

Virtuous Cycles
Other interactions result in increasingly effective information flow. In general, these interactions are characterized by:

- Open discussions, e.g. soliciting input from others, providing constructive criticism, and freely sharing new information and ideas;
- A willingness to discuss and work towards solving complex issues;
- Consideration of the goals, concerns, and knowledge bases of others.

These behaviors enable project teams to develop a better understanding of the perspectives of the other team members and use that common understanding and commitment to have open discussions about difficult topics because it is in the best interest of the project. This, in turn, results in greater productivity and satisfaction within the team.

The following example is a continuation of the earlier example, but illustrates how certain changes to the situation enabled it to morph into a virtuous cycle:

Because of the deadlock that resulted from the interaction between the owner and architect regarding the design of the high-profile exterior cladding features, the construction manager brought in an independent exterior wall system consultant to try to revive the coordination process. This consultant had studied architecture in college and had several years of experience as a contractor prior to becoming a consultant. He reviewed the drawings and issued a report with his comments and suggestions just as the owner and the owner's consultant had done earlier. However, this consultant also facilitated a series of meetings to discuss his comments. In the first meeting, he started off by explaining his technical background so that the rest of the team understood his perspective and that he had at least a working understanding of their scopes. Then he began to explain his comments. When he talked to the architect, he referred to things in architectural terms and asked the architect several questions to make sure that he understood his concerns and goals. He did the same when engaging the subcontractors and the owner. In addition to asking for clarification to make sure that he understood each party's concerns and goals, he also used his questions to link their comments to earlier comments made by others and explained how their concerns influenced aspects that were important to others. For example, during one exchange, he asked the architect, "What is the architectural intent that you are going for here? Then he asked the glazing subcontractor "How were you planning to build this condition?" He then asked the open question: "How does that (construction sequence) influence the architectural intent?" This series of questions made the contractor have to rethink their perspective from the viewpoint of the architect for a moment. He also drew critical details using three-dimensional isometrics to help the team develop a common understanding regarding the full spectrum of concerns surrounding complex issues. Gradually, the team shared information more openly and began to work productively together to collectively develop solutions that they all could comfortably commit to.

The dynamic of the team in this example was significantly different from their previous interactions. First of all, the consultant was able to build trust by demonstrating that he understood and valued the opinions of the others by bringing up issues that were of concern to them, using language familiar to them, and reinforcing their roles as experts by making them the sources of information through his questions. As a result, the team began to be more comfortable with sharing information and ideas. The consultant also took the time to explain specific issues or illustrate them with isometric sketches so that everyone could develop the same understanding of what was being discussed. By asking questions, he pulled valuable information from one person and then translated and linked that information to the goals and concern of others. This enabled the team to develop common understanding, interdependence, and a shared sense of responsibility for the outcome of their interactions. Because of these behaviors, he set in motion a virtuous cycle, where he gained the trust and developed an understanding of the various team members and then transferred that trust and understanding to the rest of the team and in the process building a common understanding and sense of mutual commitment.

This second example illustrates several behavioral dyads that help to perpetuate positive trust and learning cycles. For example, the link/build dyad and clarify/build dyad both build common understanding by either linking information from one person to another or by clarifying ambiguity. These dyads allow individuals to have more substantive discussions and continue to link and clarify new and more detailed information. There is also a dyad related to inclusivity and commitment, i.e. when individuals were asked for input or otherwise constructively involved, they felt a greater commitment to the result, shared better information, and became more active members of the team.

When asked about these positive interactions, project team members mention themes related to:

- Openness, e.g. *"We've got a fairly enlightened facilities director, so we've been able to push innovative ideas"*;
- Adaptability, e.g. *"We may be pricks, but we're reasonable pricks, so they just need to let us know if they want us to do something differently"*;
- Trust, e.g. *"The safety stuff is a bit excessive, but the safety coordinator is at all the meetings and always asks me for suggestions when I see him in the field, so I trust him"*;
- Respect and interest, e.g. *"They're the experts, I just need them to teach me enough so that I can ask the right questions"*;
- Genuine liking of each other, e.g. *"They're ahead of schedule, under budget, the work looks great, and surprisingly they actually like each other"*.

Triggers

As illustrated by these examples, there is a tremendous amount of insight that can be gained by observing project teams to understand how information behaviors develop into trends. Looking at team interactions with this perspective also makes it possible to identify the triggers that cause shifts in those trends. In fact, in terms of information flow management, identifying the triggers may be the most important insight because it provides an opportunity for teams to transcend their natural tendencies and become much more effective.

There are three main types of triggers:
1) *Individuals* who demonstrate certain socially- and technically-integrative competencies;
2) *Tools* that address the appropriate level of detail;
3) *Processes* that create psychologically stable and collaborative environments.

Individuals

As was illustrated in the second example, the exterior wall consultant was able to shift the team dynamic to one that was much more effective in terms of information flow and problem solving. Similarly, on most projects there are certain individuals who are more adept at getting the project team to understand and incorporate large amounts of new information. On one major healthcare project I was working on, there were two such individuals: a consultant who was hired to develop and implement an ambitious and innovative infection control risk assessment (ICRA) plan, and a commissioning agent was also able to implement an extensive commissioning plan. These individuals had several characteristics and competencies that made them much more effective at integrating new information into the project than other team members.

The first common characteristic was that these individuals had a strong knowledge base that consisted of both: 1) a detailed understanding of the specifics of their particular scopes and 2) a broad understanding of related scopes. Their depth of knowledge allowed them to explain the rationale behind their ideas and adapt those explanations to their audience (e.g. doctors, contractors, designers, product manufacturers, etc.). Their breadth of knowledge enabled them to translate and draw links between information contributed by others so that the new information was more meaningful to the rest of the project team.

Their strong knowledge base also gave them the confidence to solicit input from others and continuously adapt their ideas based on the new information, i.e. making them collective ideas. An interesting insight is that in almost every instance that I observed, these "trigger" individuals asked lots of questions. In fact, they asked questions more than 30% of the time as compared with less than 5% for almost all the other project team members. Through their questions, they still controlled the flow of information, but did it by "pulling" information from other project team members. Because others were providing the information, these questions helped to engage the rest of the team more deeply in the conversation and also provided a means to link that information to the concerns of others with related follow-up questions. For example, consider the interaction between a building envelope consultant, architect, and contractor described in the second example.

The consultant asked the architect what the intent was behind one specific detail. The architect said that they were going for "transparency". The consultant reiterated the architect's point and asked for confirmation by asking the rhetorical question "So you want the glass to come all the way down to the floor line?" The consultant then asked the subcontractor: "How were you thinking that you would construct this condition?" The contractor offered his thoughts and the consultant reiterated what the contractor had said, but changed some of the contractor's language into more architectural terminology. The consultant then asked the open question "How does this influence the architectural intent?"

The consultant could have simply told them how he thought the condition should be detailed, as the owner and previous consultant tried to do. However, by asking questions, he was able to simultaneously gather needed information, reinforce the role of others as the subject matter experts, build trust by valuing information provided by others, and offer solutions that were specifically developed for the unique needs of the project and project team. He was essentially able to control and manage the technical direction and social dynamic through using questions to draw the right information from others (i.e. control through guidance instead of force).

These "trigger" individuals also had a high level of emotional intelligence, i.e. an understanding of how others felt. Their ability to understand their team's subtle behaviors enabled them to: 1) know when to provide further explanation versus when additional explanation was tedious or demeaning, 2) know when and how to tactfully engage individuals who were losing interest in the discussion or hold accountable certain individuals who were making unsubstantiated claims; and 3) know how to balance the team dynamic so that the information contributions, concerns, and goals of both the soft-spoken and the more assertive team members were valued and considered.

Tools
Another trigger for improving information flow is the introduction of certain types of tools or boundary objects. The key characteristics of these tools are that they can capture the appropriate level of detail to support the development of common understanding and commitment within the team.

Boundary objects enable common understanding by serving as explicit sources of information that allow information to be viewed by all individuals at the same time and in the same form. This means that the team does not have to constantly try to recall information from past conversations or worry about whether others are accurately recalling the same information. Instead, team members can focus on the interpretation of the information directly in front of them and provide new information that is relevant to the questions at hand. One critical characteristic of these "trigger" boundary objects is that they have a structure that can capture the appropriate level of detail to support the ongoing discussions. In design and construction, something as simple as making use of three-dimensional sketches or models can drastically change the effectiveness of team interactions. As one consultant said, "*the isometrics help to smoke out the complexity*" to which another team member added "*You start drawing a 3D sketch and all of a sudden everyone's talking the same language. Even though it's a great way to see all the known information, it also makes it very obvious the things that are missing and still need to be figured out.*" While these tools captured enough detail to develop a common understanding and have substantive discussions, they also draw out questions regarding the additional information that is needed and provide a means of evaluating new information in real time. This makes them a valuable means of creating common goals (i.e. completing the information in the object) and maintaining accountability for the quality of shared information (i.e. the information needs to "fit" or make sense in the greater context).

In certain instances, boundary objects can also create a sense of shared commitment. As was mentioned previously, each project team member has certain boundary objects that are familiar or important to them. In some cases when a new entity joins a team, they introduce their own tools for the team to use. However, some individuals have much greater success in getting the project team to use their tools than others. As was mentioned in and earlier section, there was a consultant who implemented an extremely innovative and effective infection control risk assessment program. What made it so effective was that he tied the information needed for his program to the safety training program and other existing forms and processes that the subcontractors were already using. For example, they could use their own checklists and reports as long as they included certain additional information that was important to the consultant. By closely linking the consultant's tools to the subcontractor's existing tools, he was able to reduce the administrative load, pull information that was important for his scope of work, and use the tool as a means of establishing shared commitment to acquiring information that was important to the whole team.

One of the challenges with the use of tools, especially new or complex tools, is that individuals can get so caught up in using the tools that they lose sight of why that tool is important to the overall project goals. In the earlier example, although the building envelope consultant was adept at drawing quick isometric sketches to illustrate complex conditions, the architect was not. Therefore, although the coordination meetings that centered around the isometric sketches were very productive, the architect had difficulty translating the three-dimensional discussions into the design documents. After spending significant time and effort, he simply reverted back to two-dimensional sketches and much of the valuable information from the coordination meetings was lost. On another project, the team responsible for the coordination of the mechanical, electrical, and plumbing (MEP) systems used some software to combine their individual 3D fabrication drawings (i.e. building information model) and run clash detection to identify potential conflicts between systems. None of these contractors was savvy enough to use the clash detection software effectively, so they hired a full time Building Information Model (BIM) manager. In addition to fulfilling his primary role (i.e. making sure that each contractor's BIM was accurate and then combining them to run the clash report), he was also pivotal in enabling effective discussions at the coordination meetings. He was very skilled at manipulating the model in real-time. During the coordination meetings he would zoom in and out, change the angle of view, or make changes to the model fast enough to keep up with the discussion and even fuel the discussion by showing a condition in a way that generated the right questions or potential solutions. Although he was not the expert on any specific systems, through his manipulation of the model, he could often make is so that the answer was quite literally staring the rest of the team in the face.

73

Another challenge with new tools is that they can require additional administrative load, i.e. using the tool creates a whole new set of tasks that the project team needs to concern themselves with. For example, on one project, a commissioning agent introduced several new processes and forms that the subcontractors needed to fill out. Since many of the subcontractors had their own closeout processes and forms, they worked with the commissioning agent to modify the existing forms so that the same document satisfied both needs. By integrating the new tools with existing tools, they were able to keep the additional administrative load to a minimum.

By providing a manager for complex tools and by integrating new tools into existing tools and process, project teams can use new tools to improve information flow without the strain of added administrative load. These measures also allow the rest of the project team to focus on providing valuable information and make sense of new information rather than worrying about how to use the new tools.

Processes
Having the right people and tools is important, but the process for how they are brought together is just as critical. The process-based triggers that can be used to improve information flow pertain to:
- Frequency of interactions
- Collectively developed processes
- Management of expectations

Certain processes, such as those that involve frequent or intense interactions, can be used to create mutual relevance. For example, one of the most baffling things about diverse teams that meet relatively infrequently (i.e. monthly or bi-monthly) is that they spend incredible amounts of time simply reiterating the same information that was shared in the previous month's meeting. This is done so that everyone can get on the same page again; however, it leaves very little time for making decisions or sharing new information, which is the whole purpose of getting on the same page (e.g. on one project, roughly 10% of total information shared during monthly meetings was new). As one of the project managers commented, "*This is death-by-a-thousand-cuts because we can't seem to kill anything on this project – we spend all this time working toward a decision in one meeting and then all of a sudden all the options are back on the table at the next.*"

There is always some convergence of values and understanding that occurs in meetings, but as time passes without additional interactions, individuals tend to revert back to their own personal values and understandings. However, in cases where teams switch to more frequent interactions (e.g. weekly meetings), there is a lot less time spent trying to develop a common understanding and more time spent working toward solutions and discussing new information. In the case mentioned above, when the team switched to weekly meetings, roughly 50% of information shared during the meeting was new. Furthermore, in situations where teams held two or more meetings per week, the results were even more significant. In these situations, the team rarely spent any time discussing old information and in most cases had actually collaborated significantly outside of the meeting. As a result, the meetings became a forum for predominantly making decisions and discussing complex issues rather than simply sharing general information.

Another process-based factor that influences outcomes is whether the content and scope of the meeting is collectively developed versus dictated by a single individual. For example, on most construction projects there are two regular meetings where all the subcontractors and related consultants meet: the foremen's meeting and the project managers' (PM) meetings. On a healthcare project that I was involved with, these two meetings involved essentially the same individuals with the exception of the individual facilitating the meeting (i.e. the superintendant facilitated the foremen's meeting and a project manager for the general contractor facilitated the PM's meeting). While the PMs' meeting was generally regarded as frustrating and unproductive, the foremen's meeting was viewed as extremely productive and valuable. One major difference was in how the meetings were run. The PMs' meetings consisted of the PM for the general contractor running through a list of his personal concerns that he had complied into a makeshift agenda shortly before the meeting. This process resulted in very little discussion and was not well received by the subcontractors. In contrast, the foremen's meeting was much more interactive. The superintendent running the foremen's meeting had the same six major topics every meeting (i.e. safety, quality, milestones, progress updates, "old new business", and "new new business"). For each topic, the superintendent went around the table and asked each person individually if they had anything to share related to the respective topic. All of the comments were captured in the meeting minutes and used as the agenda for the following week's meeting as well as an update for other key weekly coordination meetings. This process allowed each person to share their thoughts, feel that their contributions were valued, and created a sense of collective responsibility for the outcome of the meeting. As one contractor shared, "*If something doesn't get brought up, then the rest of us can't do what it takes to get the job done – we have to look out for each other because a building like this doesn't get built without trust and respect.*"

The foremen's meeting also followed the same structure every week, so attendees knew exactly what to expect and what was expected of them. For this reason, they came prepared to share accurate and meaningful information. Processes, such as the foremen's meeting, that include some element of expectation management are significantly more productive than other meetings where attendees do not know what to expect. Part of this has to do with simply having the opportunity to prepare for a meeting, but it also has to do with creating a level of psychological safety. In situations where individuals know what to expect, they can focus on listening, learning, and using their constantly-changing understanding to contribute relevant information to the discussion. In psychologically unsafe environments, individuals have to constantly protect and promote their own interests and cannot objectively interpret new information in a timely enough manner to make valuable contributions.

By understanding the key moderators affecting information flow, their interrelation, and the triggers that result in positive or negative iterations of trust and learning cycles, managers can develop awareness and eventually a proficiency at facilitating interactions so that valuable information is made available and understood. The following chapter discusses how managers can make sure that once information has been shared by the project team, it is incorporated into the project through more effective decision-making.

Chapter 4

Decision Making & Ambiguity

Trust and learning are vital in getting information to flow, but the whole purpose is to get it to flow in the right direction so that it benefits the project. As was mentioned in Chapter 1, it is only when information is captured in a decision that it truly adds value to the project.

The Hambrick and Mason model for decision making for conditions of bounded rationality (1984) discussed in Chapter 2 showed how decision-makers rely on their values and mental models to filter through the massive amounts of information available so that they can focus on the most important pieces of information to make decisions. In a collaborative environment where decisions are collectively made, individuals need to have similar enough filters so that they can reach a common decision and collectively be committed to it. While the trust and learning cycles provide a means for facilitating shifts in values and mental models, in order for change to occur, there has to be some level of conflict. Conflict occurs when two differing forces interact and, as a result of their interaction, at least one is left fundamentally different than it was before the interaction. In team interactions, conflict is created when different individuals with their differing values and mental models have to arrive at a common decision.

So what exactly is conflict? In organizational science, conflict is often defined as: 1) an opposition in goals, aims, and values between different entities (Dirks and McLean Parks, 2003; 285);

2) competition over scarce resources such as influence, money, or time (Pondy, 1967); or 3) a necessary part of good decision making (e.g. as in a quote attributed to General George S. Patton Jr., "if everyone is thinking alike, then someone isn't thinking").

Conflict is not inherently good or bad, but simply a matter of differences. In her pioneering research on the topic (1941), Mary Parker Follett outlined three ways of dealing with these differences:

- *Domination,* which requires other entities to adjust to the dominating individual's mental model and values. Although this is often immediately effective, it is not always successful over the long term due to the negative side effects that diminish trust and commitment;
- *Compromise,* which requires that both parties change and consciously give up something so that the activity can continue. Depending on the characteristics of the interaction, these compromises may be viewed as lose/lose or win/win;
- *Integration,* which allows both sides to achieve their full goals but depends on the full situation being understood by both parties and each entity's demands being broken down into their constituent parts (i.e. transparency and learning).

In collaborative team environments where decisions are made collectively, it is clearly preferred to use integration or "win/win" type compromise. However, the ability of the team to use these means depends on the type of conflict that exists within the team.

To aid in understanding the nuances of conflict, social science research has identified three major types of conflict:

- *Substantive Conflict*, or differences in viewpoints, opinions, or general approaches to a task (Pelled et al, 1999; Jehn and Mannix, 2001); 2)
- *Affective Conflict*, orpersonality or interpersonal conflict characterized by anger, frustration, or uneasiness (Pelled et al., 1999; Walton and Dutton, 1969);
- *Process Conflict*, or conflict over how something should be done concerning duty, responsibility, accountability, or resource delegation (Jehn 1997; Jehn et al., 1999).

The predominant predictor of substantive conflict is diversity which can be evaluated in terms of demographic type (age, ethnicity, gender, etc.) or in terms of information type (functional area, level of education, tenure with firm, etc.) (Jehn et al., 1997; Jehn et al., 1999). Substantive conflict is mainly technical in nature and has been shown to lead to positive task-related outcomes such as decision comprehensiveness (Simons et al., 1999), constructive communications (Lovelace et al., 2001), task progress and efficiency (Tjosvold, 1997, Wong et al., 1992), and improved individual performance (Jehn, 1994, Shah and Jehn, 1993). These benefits are even greater for non-routine tasks such as many of the discussions that occur on construction projects (Jehn, 1995).

Affective conflict is also increased by demographic diversity (Jehn et al., 1997) and functional background diversity (Pelled et al., 1999) but is more personal in nature. Studies have shown that affective conflict has detrimental effects on the free and open exchange of information and other relational outcomes such as satisfaction, commitment and cohesiveness, respect, and trust (Earley & Moskowski 2000, Jehn and Mannix, 2001; Jehn 1994; 1995; 1997; Jehn et al., 1999). It also has a negative effect on task-related outcomes such as perceived performance, actual performance, and efficacy of communicative and planning activities (Earley and Moskowski, 2000; Shah and Jehn, 1993; Jehn, 1994; Jehn et al., 1999). Trust moderates the extent that substantive conflict translates into affective conflict. For example, in low trust situations, much of the substantive conflict translates into detrimental affective conflict, but in high trust situations there is neutral or positive interpretation of the substantive conflict that prevents its translation into affective conflict (Simons & Peterson, 2000). Also, individuals in high-trust relationships tend to evaluate their relationships with much longer time metrics than those in low-trust relationships and therefore are willing to overlook a single negative incident more readily (Holmes & Rempel, 1989).

Similar to affective conflict, unresolved process conflict also tends to have a negative effect on task outcomes because of the frustration and confusion related to what, how, and when activities are supposed to be performed. However, instead of directly affecting performance, process conflict mostly manifests itself as reduced commitment (which has an indirect influence on the quality of work). In addition, unresolved process conflict has other relational outcomes such as increased likelihood of leaving, role ambiguity, perceived unfairness, and decreased cohesiveness, trust, respect, and satisfaction (Jehn, 1997; Jehn et al., 1999; Jehn and Mannix, 2001). The combination of high affective and process conflict can be especially detrimental. In these cases, parties clash personally while also disagreeing about responsibilities and accountability. This is illustrated in the excerpt from Dirks and McLean Parks below (2003: 302):

"The combination of high affective and process conflict and high substantive conflict over a non-routine task may be particularly deadly. In this situation, high affective and process conflict results in personal clashes among the parties (affective conflict) who are unwilling or unable to specify responsibilities and accountability (process conflict). Information will be hoarded,

ideas will be suppressed, and the high levels of conflict on all fronts will result in fractious and contentious discussions. As a result, the group is unlikely to resolve their differences and performance is likely to suffer."

Conflict is a natural part of collaboration. While differing perspectives of a situation create conflict, several other factors affect whether that conflict translates into positive or negative outcomes (the social dynamic within the group, the presence or absence of trust, etc.). In turn, the type of conflict has significant effects on an individual's commitment to the project, commitment to the team, future information sharing, and role in the team social dynamic.

So, how can conflict be managed so that a collaborative team experiences the benefits of substantive conflict without the detrimental aspects of affective conflict and unresolved process conflict? Arguably, the most critical factor is effective management of ambiguity.

Ambiguity

Each individual in a team may have different values and knowledge bases, but what brings these differences to light is when multiple individuals have to interpret the same ambiguous situation. How they manage the ambiguity is at the heart of managing conflict. In particular, there are two major considerations for managing ambiguity: 1) understanding the type of situation and 2) understanding the type of ambiguity.

In terms of the type of situation, Mischel (1977) made a distinction between "weak" and "strong" situations. Weak situations are when the environmental stimulus (i.e. the need for action) is fairly mild and there are many possible courses of action. In these situations, individuals make decisions based on their personal interpretations, past experiences (Cyert &

March, 1963), actions that are familiar to them (Axelrod, 1976), or actions that reflect their functional backgrounds (Kimberly & Evanisko, 1981). In contrast, "strong" situations have very strong environmental stimuli (e.g. there is a fire!!!) and the possible courses of action are relatively clear (e.g. put it out or run). In these types of situations, the strength of the situation requires individuals set aside their personal perspectives in the interest of coming to a quick and appropriate common decision regarding the critical issue.

The other factor influencing the type of conflict is the type of ambiguity. In looking at hundreds of team conflict situations, there were over twenty different types of ambiguity that emerged over and over again. However, for the sake of simplicity, these can be narrowed down to five basic types:

- *Goal Ambiguity:* Goals are the overall motivating factor for project team members. However, among the team it is often unclear how each person understands and interprets the: 1) *Overall project goals*; 2) *Individual project goals*, and 3) *Individual personal goals.*

- *Approach Ambiguity:* "Approach" is used to denote the general philosophy that governs team decision-making. This involves the: 1) *Level of risk* that one is comfortable with; 2) *Level of innovation* one is willing to pursue; 3) *Prioritization of goals* to serve as a basis for decision-making; and 4) *Process for achieving goals*, i.e. understanding how various activities fit together and into the context of the overall project.

- *Role/Responsibility Ambiguity:* Roles are important because they define each person's identity within the team. Roles empower people to be responsible for certain scopes of information and also define the social and technical relationships that fuel the team dynamic. The major subcategories are: 1) *Formal Role*, i.e. per contract; 2) *Informal Role* based on actual expertise; 3) *Social Role*, i.e.

the role that they play in group dynamics; 4) *Discretion,* authority to make decisions; 5) *Motivational Role,* i.e. what inspires people to perform; 6) *Contextual Role,* e.g. understanding how each person fits into the context of the others and interdependencies between them, and 7) *Expectations* of individual performance or behavior.

- *Critical Issues Ambiguity*: This deals with the understanding the effect that one decision has on other decisions. While this type of ambiguity may be different for different domains, in construction this involves understanding how various decisions impact each other with regard to: 1) *Different dimensions,* e.g. three spatial dimensions, sequencing, cost, performance, aesthetics, and contracts; 2) *Scale,* e.g. how does a decision related to one specific area of a project influence the entire project, the entire campus, the entire master plan, and the community; and 3) *Constancy,* e.g. making sure that new decisions are consistent with past decisions.

- *Validity/Appropriateness Ambiguity*: This also may vary from one domain to another, but has to do with understanding the quality of specific information contributions and their appropriateness to the given situation (e.g. is the comment that the mechanical engineer just made valid).

Hierarchy of Ambiguity
Every interaction includes some sort of ambiguity and that ambiguity results in some sort of conflict. While some instances of conflict can be productive and result in valuable collaboration, other instances can be extremely unproductive and frustrating and result in detrimental team performance. One of the major factors in determining the difference between productive and unproductive conflict is whether the team discussions target the appropriate level of ambiguity.

There are certain fundamental issues that require a common understanding and commitment in order to have substantive discussions about more specific issues. For example, without agreeing upon the goal of a project, it is difficult to develop or evaluate an approach for achieving that goal. In this example, if the discussion is focused on debating what approach should be taken without clarity in terms of goals, then the discussion will be frustrating and relatively unproductive. Although everyone may have thoughts and opinions about the best approach, their reasoning is based on their notion of what they think the goals should be. This unaddressed ambiguity about goals is what results in frustration and unproductive conflict. In these cases, one individual may feel that another team member is not working toward the "team goal" (or his notion of what the team goal should be), when ironically the other team member feels that she is working toward the "team goal" (again, her personal, and often unsaid, notion of what the team goal should be). Both individuals feel that their efforts are being ignored or rejected by the other person. The unaddressed goal-related ambiguity causes a vicious cycle that frames the approach-related discussions as harmful conflict that will negatively affect information flow within the team.

If the team first establishes a clear goal, however, then they can use the same basis for evaluating arguments for various approaches and focus their attention on clarifying ambiguity related to the approach. Similarly, once the approach is clarified, then there can be substantive discussions about roles and responsibilities. Once the roles and responsibilities have been clarified, there can be more substantive and respectful discussions regarding critical issues and the validity of information. Essentially, this suggests that there is a hierarchy of ambiguity (see Figure 12) where more fundamental issues (i.e. levels 1-3) need to be addressed before there can be substantive discussions regarding more specific issues (i.e. levels 4 and 5).

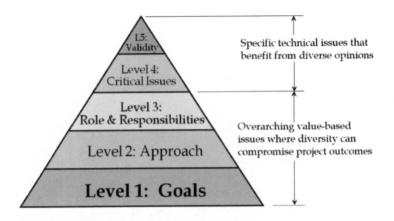

Figure 12: Hierarchy of Ambiguity

Most of the discussions that project teams have are related to debating ambiguity levels 4 and 5. However, in cases where there is also unaddressed ambiguity related to levels 1 through 3, these discussions end up creating the type of conflict that compromises the team's ability to have productive discussions about level 4 and 5 issues. This is not to say that teams should not disagree or debate. Intellectual conflict and diversity of opinions regarding critical issues and validity are necessary to providing quality information to the project. However, without clarifying more fundamental issues, these discussions also hit upon more personal and value-based issues and can negatively affect trust, commitment, and the effectiveness of future interactions. For these reasons, targeting the appropriate level of ambiguity is one of the most critical factors affecting the outcome of the trust and learning cycles. The following cases illustrate the value in being able to manage ambiguity.

The Children's Hospital Design Review Meeting: Getting the "Dummy of the Day" Award

During the early part of the design phase for a children's hospital, a major meeting with over twenty high-profile attendees was held at the architect's office. The goal of this meeting was to review the entire design effort to date and provide feedback to the designers. The morning was spent reviewing the different floor plans and making decisions on what to do about certain spaces. However, at some points in the discussion, issues emerged for which there was not a clear expert, so in essence everyone thought they were the expert and strongly pushed their own uneducated opinions. One of these topics was the linen cart storage space on the first floor. The team spent over 30 minutes trying to figure out what to do about this space. Different individuals presented very impassioned arguments as to the preferences of the linen cart handlers (none of those present had ever actually solicited any input from the linen cart handlers). Finally, the discussion was dropped without conclusion because it wasn't going anywhere and everyone was getting very frustrated with each other.

In this first part of this meeting (described above), there were a couple of characteristics that kept the discussions from being productive. Firstly, there was no clear goal in terms of what was needed from this aspect of the design (i.e. what would be most valuable to the end users). Second, there were no means of evaluating various options (i.e. no clarity on approach). Third, there was no clear authority on the matter (i.e. ambiguity regarding roles). These factors combined to create a situation where each person (e.g. the head of nursing) felt that they were the resident expert in linen cart storage preferences. However, her opinion was based on her personal preferences and ambiguous understanding of the goals, approach, and roles of the other project team members. When others (e.g. the head of facilities) commented on her ideas or presented alternate ideas, these comments not only conflicted with the head of nursing's ideas on a technical level, but also conflicted with her unstated personal goals and interpretation of what was important to the project. Subsequently, she would respond in kind with dismissive comments about the ideas presented by others and this only perpetuated these personal differences. This created significant affective conflict and set up a negative environment for interpretation of new information. Without having clarity regarding goals, approach, and roles, there was no basis for discussing the technical merits of various ideas.

After the debacle with the floor plan review, the conversation moved to the review of the exterior design of the building. When architects put their rendering of the children's hospital up on the wall, initially, the same types of unfounded comments that had plagued many parts of the morning discussion began to emerge again (i.e. personal preferences, uneducated opinions, etc.). For example, one of the administrators for the hospital made the comment, "Everyone likes trees, but I just think that the trees on the rendering are too big". Thankfully, just as the architect started to explain about the size of the virtual trees, the chief campus planner from the medical center stepped in and asked some very important questions. The chief planner was a soft-spoken man with a self-deprecating sense of humor but an amazing ability to cut very clearly to the heart of an issue. He started off – "Maybe I get the dummy of the day award, but what is the intent of the design?" The architect explained the qualitative and quantitative goals of the design. The chief planner then asked about the different materials that made up the wall systems and what their significance was in helping to realize the architectural intent. The design architect answered his questions and elaborated on some of the issues to explain further. The chief planner and others built on the architect's answers and very constructive discussion ensued.

The main difference in this second session was the series of questions asked by the chief planner. His questions came across as genuine even though he had a detailed understanding of architectural theory. He asked them because he was interested in understanding the architect's thoughts and perspective on this specific project. Also, the systematic and incremental manner that he asked his questions helped the others understand the basis for the design and converge on their understanding of what the architecture was supposed to convey. In addition, his asking questions also empowered the architects (as the subject matter expert) to explain their thoughts and goals behind the design that were not clear to the group earlier. This series of questions and comments enabled others to understand the architectural goals and the how these goals were incorporated into the design and helped to reinforce the architect's role and illustrate the depth of thought that had already gone into the current design. Now the group had a much clearer basis for addressing the critical issues regarding the exterior wall design and the foundation for constructive debate and discussion.

The Cancer Institute Value Engineering Session: Finding $30 Million in 36 hours

At two points during the cancer institute delivery process, it became clear that the projected budget was significantly over the target budget. To address this issue, the owner's representative facilitated a two-day intensive value engineering session with the goal of cutting $30 million out of a current estimate of $160 million while maintaining as much value as possible. The owner's representative invited all individuals involved with the Cancer Institute project to attend: key design professionals, key consultants, hospital administrators, contractors, facilities personnel, and representatives from various user groups. The impetus for these meetings was to reconcile the scope of work reflected in the current drawings with the target budget. These meetings were set up as two full days back-to-back with everyone in the same room. The general sequence of events proceeded as follows:

- The owner's rep began by reviewing the project process map that he had created which included the major goals for each phase;

- The owner's rep explained that the overall goal of the meeting was to bring the project back within the target budget while maintaining as much value as possible. In this case, the group needed to cut $30 million out to maintain the original $130 million budget;

- He then gave an overview of the process for the two-day meeting (i.e. the sequence of activities and their significance to the overall goal).

- The owner's rep went around the room and asked each person to introduce him/herself and share their main personal concerns and goals for the meeting, and he wrote them on the wall where everyone could see them for the duration of the two-day session;

- Everyone reviewed the current design and the two estimates provided by the construction manager and the architect's cost consultant. Discrepancies between the two budgets were reconciled.

- The group broke into smaller groups charged with focusing on a certain scope of work. This usually consisted of an exterior cladding/site work/interiors group and a mechanical/plumbing/electrical systems group. Each group was responsible for developing a list of options to be considered for value engineering.

- The two groups reconvened as one large group and they debated and modified the developed options until they brought the budget back to the target amount.

The beauty of these sessions is that all the decision-makers were present; these included the principals of the various design firms and the administrators of the hospital. These were the people who had the knowledge to evaluate options and the discretion to make decisions. In addition, there was a strong tangible goal and an understanding of the overarching priority: meet the budget first and then incorporate as much value as possible. The daunting nature of the goal and the short intense period of time in which it had to be accomplished (i.e. two days) created a strong situation and a sense of shared fate. Coupled with the initial sharing of personal goals and concerns, this created an atmosphere where the goals for the meeting governed over personal goals, but the personal goals (that were posted on the wall) had to be taken into account in order to develop solutions that could be agreed upon. The transparency of reviewing the budgets line by line provided a means for letting others learn about the cost impacts of various design features and helped develop trust in the estimates and estimators by checking numbers and getting additional feedback. Trust in the estimators was critical for the next day's discussions regarding evaluation of the various value-engineering options and making final decisions. The use of breakout groups also enabled better cohesion of individuals interested in specific scope areas (i.e. more initial overlap of values and mental models). This enabled more focused and interesting discussions. In addition, although there was an overall goal for the two-day meeting of reconciling the actual budget with the target budget, the event was structured such that each section of the meeting had its own sub-goals that fed into the overall goals in order to maintain motivation and momentum, but also to ensure that the groups were being held accountable for working toward the final outcome.

These two examples illustrate how managing ambiguity can enable teams to make more effective use of their collective knowledge by minimizing destructive conflict. The management of ambiguity, in addition to 1) understanding the underlying structure and characteristics of information flow and 2) enabling positive iterations of trust and learning, are the three most critical components to effectively managing information flow. They have strong implications for managing teams at several levels. The first is at the interaction level, i.e. getting individuals to share, discuss, and collaboratively develop ideas and solve problems. This has been the primary focus up to this point. The second level is looking at the delivery process, i.e. making sure that the right people, tools, and processes are incorporated at the right time to optimize the value to the project. Chapter 5 will focus on this. Finally, there are implications for managing the overall context of the project, i.e. having organizational structures and strategies in place that are appropriate for the project environment and support efforts at the delivery process and interaction levels. This will be discussed further in Chapter 6.

Chapter 5

Information Flow Management

There is a clever poem by Sam Walter Foss entitled "The Calf Path". In this poem he describes how long ago a calf was just aimlessly wandering through the woods. The next day, a dog followed the path the calf had taken and then a flock of sheep followed suit. At this point, the winding path had become a trail and people began to use it even though they constantly complained about how crooked it was. Eventually it became a road, then a street. One hundred and fifty years later, it had turned into a main thoroughfare for a busy metropolis and the crookedness and inefficiency of the path now were experienced by thousands of people daily simply because it always seemed easier to keep using something that was already there rather than come up with something better. As Sam Walter Foss eloquently writes:

> *"For men are prone to go it blind,*
> *Along the calf-paths of the mind;*
> *And work away from sun to sun,*
> *To do what other men have done."*

One of the common pitfalls in any kind of process is that individuals tend to do things "just because" someone long ago, without the perspective of the needs of today, made decisions to do it that way. There have been countless times when I've asked individuals why they do their work a certain way and they respond, "Look, I've been doing it this way for 30 years." There is usually some inherent wisdom in tradition and familiarity in not constantly "reinventing the wheel". However, without periodic reflection and evaluation, our established processes end up being nothing more than habits that are no longer relevant to the needs of today. When we do things "just because" we build a trap that bounds and limits our potential in the future. While there are efficiencies to be gained from familiarity, it is necessary to balance that with periodic reflection to evaluate whether the familiar process still provides the right type of value for the effort.

This chapter develops a process for information flow planning and management. It builds on the Lean Production movement made famous by Toyota and seminal books such as "The Machine that Changed the World" (Womack and Jones, 1991), "The Toyota Way" (Liker, 2003) and "Lean Thinking" (Womack and Jones, 1996). Lean production has heavily influenced manufacturing in the last few decades as the Toyota Production System (TPS) and other continuous process improvement techniques have permeated into the mainstream business consciousness. Lean philosophy outlines five basic steps for understanding what process steps create value or waste and how the process can be continually improved. These steps consist of:

1) *Specifying value* as defined by the end customers;
2) Identifying the *value stream* and the specific actions for the process;
3) Making the value-creating steps *flow* toward the end product;
4) Letting the end users *pull* the end product through the value stream;
5) *Pursuing perfection* in every aspect.

These systems work wonderfully for repetitive processes in controlled environments, where complexity, uncertainty, and interdependence can be anticipated relatively easily. The repetition provides continuous opportunity to identify variations in quality or productivity and then learn from the negative or positive aspects of those variations to improve future iterations. However, when lean principles are applied to the delivery of a one-time, one-of-a-kind product (e.g. a construction project), the lessons from one project require a much deeper level of understanding so that they can be generalized, interpreted, and adapted to other projects. This requires something that has been very difficult for our industry to accomplish: continuous, incremental, and methodical improvement across projects. Through the Lean Construction Institute (www.leanconstruction.org) and many academic research initiatives across the country, lean principles have begun to permeate into construction industry practices, however, the focus has been primarily on labor and materials flows (i.e. flows governed by technical characteristics) and not the underlying socio-technical information flows that enable and inform everything else on the project.

This chapter takes the socio-technical concepts described in the previous chapters and integrates it with the lean production management philosophy. The result is a framework that project managers can use to develop detailed information flow plans that they can then use to manage and continuously improve their work.

Defining Value

The most important step in developing any type of process is defining "value". Defining value is often overlooked because the notion of what is valuable is assumed to be understood. In fact, at the mere mention of "vision statements" or "goals defining session" most individuals roll their eyes and prepare for a long, abstract discussion that they believe will result, ironically, in very little value. The problem is that the notion of "value" is typically either: 1) left as something that is too abstract and difficult to meaningfully apply to a project (e.g. "we want to create a 'sense of place'"); or 2) translated into an actionable goal that may not adequately address the real needs of the end users (e.g. using something such as Leadership in Energy and Environmental Design (LEED) certification as a proxy for providing a healthier and more productive indoor environment). These two prevalent challenges stem from one major disconnect: there is very little understanding of how the day-to-day actions of the project team translate into value for the end-user.

The first challenge is to understand what is of value to the end user or client. Since many clients are not that savvy in terms of the design and production process, they often do not know what they really want or the full spectrum of options available to them. For these reasons, it is often necessary for project teams to go beyond what the client asks for to understand what they really want.

Market research and product developers have methods for eliciting what users really want (e.g. observing focus group behaviors, surveys, letting users test prototypes and alternate prototypes, conjoint analyses, etc.). However, these methods are mostly focused on consumer products rather than major building projects, there are some valuable insights to be gained. One example is a very innovative process used by the architecture firm of L.D. Astorino in Pittsburgh, PA to establish the design intent for a children's hospital. Usually, children's hospital designers establish the design intent by conducting future needs and planning studies to establish spatial requirements, interview various user groups to get "wish lists" and qualitative descriptors, and benchmark against design trends in similar buildings. While this process usually gives the user groups and hospital what they asked for, it often falls short of giving them what they truly wanted. Without linking these individual preferences to an overarching design philosophy, project teams often end up with a complex hybrid of different goals that make it difficult to provide consistent decision making (similar to the witty notion of a "camel" being the result of a "horse designed by committee").

Often it is necessary for designers to go beyond "the voice of the customer" in order to effectively define value. One means of doing this is to focus on "the behavior of the customer" (i.e. understanding how they actually behave). A classic case for this is the Oxo measuring cup. When trying to figure out a better design for the measuring cup, the design team observed people actually using measuring cups. What they realized was that whenever someone puts liquid in the cup, they then lift it up to look at the graduations on the side of the cup to know whether more needs to be added. This extra step does not add any value to what the customer is trying to achieve. If you ask customers what they want, they may say larger numbers, more gradations, etc., but what they were really looking for is greater ease in reading measurements. So, Oxo designed a cup where the graduations can be seen from above, so that as someone is pouring liquid into the cup, he can immediately see the volume without having to lift the cup. By studying behavior, the design team was able to get more to the heart of what constituted value to the end user.

When behaviors are straightforward and relatively simple, they are easy to observe and easy to gain insight from. However, in complex buildings, behaviors are too numerous, complicated, and often contradictory to effectively inform the project team. In these cases it is necessary to get beyond both the "voice of the customer" and the "behavior of the customer" to the "mind of the customer" to really understand what is valuable. L.D. Astorino tried this approach when they were charged with the design of a children's hospital. They hired the consulting firm of Olson Zaltman Associates to facilitate a process called ZMET (Zaltman Metaphor Elicitation Technique). This process involves a series of interviews with user group representatives. Prior to those meetings, the users are asked to find images that represent their thoughts and feelings about a given topic (i.e. in this case, what a children's hospital should be). The use of images allows individuals to bypass the constraints of words and get to hidden and more subconscious thoughts. Through analysis of these images and the explanations that the interviewees give, ZMET gives designers insight as to the essence of what the users really want. In the case of the hospital design, the three underlying metaphors were: Control, Community, and Transformation. When the designers developed their concepts based on these three metaphors and presented them back to the user groups, the users loved them; the design team was able to cut through tremendous complexity and get to the heart of what was truly of value to the users.

Goals and Strategies

Understanding "value" to the end user is a critical first step, however, translating that value into something that is actionable for the project team is another challenge altogether. This translational step is a major stumbling block for many teams and a point where a lot of value can be instantly lost. The difficulty is that the goals of the end users and goals of the project team are focused on different things. End users are thinking about usability, maintenance, durability, aesthetics, safety, etc., while project teams are thinking about the different materials, systems, how they come together, how they look, how much they cost, etc. In order to keep value from being lost in translation, clients and project teams need to develop a joint understanding of each other's goals. In this book, I make a distinction between goals and strategies. Goals refer to value to the client (e.g. having a high market value), whereas strategies are the mechanisms that the project team uses to deliver value (e.g. architecturally significance, design awards, flexibility in future tenant fit-out). The key to project success is making sure that the appropriate strategies are selected to effectively and efficiently deliver value to the end user.

Glenn Bell, CEO of the consulting engineering firm of Simpson Gumpertz & Heger, has a very simple but powerful equation for value: Value=Performance/Cost. While the equation itself is essentially a cost-benefit analysis, the real significance is in defining the different types of performance and cost and the relationships between them that allow for the maximization of value.

Performance can be thought of in terms of three basic aspects: 1) Functionality (i.e. what does it do?), 2) Effectiveness (i.e. how well does it do it?), and 3) Durability (i.e. how long can it do it effectively?). Performance can also be evaluated in terms of the performance of the project team (e.g. coordination, budget, schedule, and quality), the performance of the physical building (e.g. aesthetics, management of structural, heat, air, and moisture loadings, durability, etc.), and the performance of the building occupants (e.g. efficiency in work flow, satisfaction, indoor air quality, etc.).

There are also three main aspects to cost: 1) Economic Cost (i.e. the monetary flows required to design, construct, operate, and maintain the building), 2) Environmental Cost (i.e. the non-monetary inputs and outputs related to materials, energy, chemicals, and emissions that affect the indoor and surrounding outdoor environment), and 3) Social Cost (i.e. the negative impact or missed opportunity in terms of positive impact that the building has upon the community). Each of these costs can be evaluated in the context of the initial design and construction of the building (i.e. initial cost) or over the entire life cycle of the building (i.e. long-term cost).

For any given project, an owner may have one or several of these aspects that feed into their goals. For example, institutional owners may be interested in minimizing the long-term economic cost of the building by focusing on durable materials, high-efficiency systems, and a layout that can easily be adapted to meet future needs. However, when project teams look at a project, they need to translate the owner's goals into a specific strategy. In many cases, there are certain strategies that may effectively address one aspect of the value definition, but compromise other aspects. For example, some high-performance mechanical systems may increase initial economic cost to the project, but decrease long-term economic and environmental cost. On the other hand, there may be passive energy efficiency measures that do not increase initial economic cost but still decrease long-term economic and environmental cost (e.g. thoughtful placement of glazing assemblies or building layout to respond to climate and seasonal considerations).

Based on the definition of Value=Performance/Cost, value can be increased by increasing performance or by decreasing costs. There are some design and construction strategies that, when executed properly, clearly increase value. There are also strategies that may increase both performance and cost or decrease both. In these cases, more in-depth analyses are needed to determine the true cost or benefit to the project. Some of the strategies that have been shown to consistently add value when executed properly include: 1) high-performance sustainable design, 2) use of building information modeling, and 3) integrated project delivery.

High-performance sustainable design requires intimate knowledge of natural and physical phenomena and uses that knowledge to create a building that: 1) controls natural processes (i.e. manages beneficial processes, and protects against disruptive ones), 2) supplements natural processes with appropriate artificial processes, and 3) manages the interaction, controllability, and feedback loops between related natural and artificial process. The value "balance sheet" for high-performance sustainable design strategies shows: 1) increased performance of the physical building and user comfort and health, 2) increased performance of project team resulting from close coordination with related scopes and subsequent learning, 3) increased performance within the community due to greater awareness of how the built environment can positively influence the natural environment, 4) decreased cost for operational and maintenance inputs throughout the life of the building, and 5) decreased risk of sub-optimal occupant productivity due to increased user comfort and health (Horman et al, 2006). There are those who contend that there is a higher initial economic cost associated with high-performance strategies, but in most cases, the additional cost is due to ineffective integration of sustainability strategies into the delivery process.

In recent years, one very promising means of improving coordination that has emerged is the development of well-thought out building information modeling (BIM) protocols into projects. BIM is a parametric modeling protocol that ties several dimensions of information (e.g. cost, schedule, etc.) to a 3D model so that when design changes are made to the model, the schedule and budget impacts can also be evaluated. BIM is still in the relatively early stages of its development within the industry and our understanding of its full potential is still limited; however, BIM has already been shown to: 1) increase project performance through faster and higher quality installation of coordinated systems; 2) enhance the understanding of one's own systems and others' systems through closer interaction with other project team members; 3) decreased social cost due to fewer field conflicts that also results in lower economic cost; and 4) decreased life-cycle cost due to involvement of facilities managers in the process, reducing their learning curve in understanding the systems, and providing insight that helps to reduce long-term maintenance costs (CIFE 2007). Efforts such as the Association of General Contractors BIMForum and the American Institute of Architects' Technology in Architectural Practice Group have encouraged the industry to continuously push the limits of BIM and how it can provide value to project teams.

Another means of fostering greater collaboration within project teams is through the use of various integrated delivery methods. Integrated project delivery (IPD), in the general sense, involves strategies and structures designed to provide greater interaction and integration between project team members (e.g. designers, contractors, owners, vendors, and user groups). These types of contractual arrangements (e.g. design-build, consortia, joint ventures, partnerships, and formal IPD contracts) allow for more information to be available throughout the delivery process and enable greater collaboration between project team members. Integrated delivery methods have been shown to improve the long-term performance of the firms involved through greater learning and professional development, stronger and more positive relationships with other firms, and greater chance of follow-on work with the project team members on future projects. Studies of design-build projects have shown improved performance through more effective incorporation of ideas, such as sustainability strategies, innovative design or construction features, or new equipment and systems (Pulaski et al., 2003). The effective incorporation of these strategies also results in decreased economic and environmental cost during the project and the life of the building. Integrated project delivery, such as design-build, has also been shown to result in projects that are of higher quality, finished on or ahead of schedule, and below budget (Konchar and Sanvido, 1998).

The above strategies are only truly value-adding when executed effectively. Issues such as poor coordination or selection of strategies that are poorly aligned with owner goals can reduce the performance and increase the cost to the point where they negatively impact project success. There are also several strategies that have the potential to be value-adding, but need to carefully balance the increases in performance with the corresponding increase in cost. Strategies such as designing for durability, pursuing LEED certification, and design for future flexibility are just a few that fall into this category. In some cases, these strategies are viewed as ways to add significant value while in other cases these may be considered wasted time, money, and effort. The dilemma with these strategies is two-fold and underscores the fundamental problems facing project teams, specifically: 1) Selection, i.e. how do project teams make sure that selected strategies are aligned with the end users' notion of value, and 2) Process management, i.e. how do teams execute these strategies efficiently and effectively?

Strategy Selection
There are countless strategies that a project team could choose to pursue. Project teams interested in improving constructability could focus on strategies that decrease schedule, utilize prefabrication, improve coordination, etc. Similarly, teams interested in sustainability can select various strategies that focus on reducing environmental impact, creating high performance systems, integrating various systems to reduce redundancy, etc. If creating a building of high architectural significance is the primary goal, then the project team will target strategies to create a building that will be a landmark for the community and influence the notion of what a building can be. There are countless other types of strategies that can be developed depending on the project goals (e.g. adaptive reuse, designing for future flexibility, community involvement, etc.). One very progressive firm, Tocci Building Corporation in Woburn, MA has a Virtual Design and Construction Group that has developed 96 different strategies related to BIM, and depending on the project goals, they can select and integrate the right mix of strategies.

This brings up a critical question: With all of these potential strategies, how do teams select the most appropriate strategies that best align with the owner's notion of value? If there are only a handful of strategies that a team can execute effectively, then the decision may be fairly easy. However, if the firms involved have a large number of well thought-out strategies available to them, then it may necessary for them to categorize and classify them so that they can more easily select the suite of strategies that are most appropriate for a particular project. One useful means of developing this type of system is to create a master matrix that lists all their potentials and rates each strategy based on how well it addresses the spectrum of performance and cost goals in which owners could be interested (e.g. 0 for no correlation, 5 for a very strong correlation, with positive correlations as positive numbers and negative correlations as negative numbers). This essentially creates something similar to a House of Quality matrix. Once this matrix is developed, the team can assign weights (e.g. on a scale of 0-1) to each of the performance and cost metrics based on their importance to the project and very quickly narrow down the appropriate strategies that should be further explored on the specific project. Other formalized techniques, such as "Choosing by Advantages", build upon this same basic methodology to enable transparent and consistent decision-making.

Tactics

Once the team has agreed upon a common strategy or set of strategies then they can begin to plan out the tactics (i.e. the specific sets of activities that allow project teams to execute strategies). One example of this is the US Green Building Council's LEED program. Despite its limitations, one of its greatest contributions to the construction industry is that it provides a fairly comprehensive list of sustainability-related tactics. Depending on the project goals, the project team can select the tactics that are most appropriate. One challenge for LEED is that getting the certification often becomes more important than actually delivering a sustainable building and therefore in some cases it addresses the owner's goals related to "marketability" rather than "sustainability".

I did some work with the predecessor to LEED for Healthcare Facilities (the Green Guide for Health Care). I took each of its +200 credits (i.e. tactics) and developed a detailed list of the sequence of activities needed to effectively achieve each credit, essentially creating a workflow. For each activity, I assigned an optimal phase (e.g. master planning, schematic design, preconstruction, construction, etc.) and elements of responsibility (i.e. the individuals who are primarily responsible, need to be involved, or need to be aware of the activity). Once the appropriate credits were selected, the database could be sorted by phase and entity (e.g. architect, general contractor, mechanical engineer, glazing subcontractor, etc) to develop custom process maps and custom descriptions of the roles and responsibilities for each entity through the various phases of project delivery. This is just one method for beginning to plan and manage the flow of value. While there are countless ways that this can be accomplished, the main point is that project teams need to place greater emphasis on understanding and managing their processes and associated information flows.

Process Management
Process management has to begin with understanding existing processes. Process mapping out a sequence of activities into a workflow provides a good starting point for analysis. There are several well-established methodologies and techniques for process mapping that are not elaborated upon here. At its most basic level, a process map is a series of interrelated activities on a timeline, but it is also important to incorporate elements such as: 1) Level of detail, i.e. some processes are more detailed subsets of overarching processes but it is important to capture both detail and context (see Figure 14); and 2) Responsibilities; i.e. understanding who needs to be involved with each activity and who is primarily responsible for each activity through the use of "swim lanes" or activity involvement boxes (Figure 15) informs coordination, timing of involvement, and contractual relationships.

Level 1

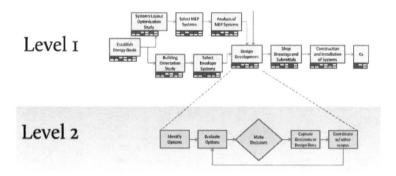

Level 2

Figure 14: Example of Mapping Level of Detail

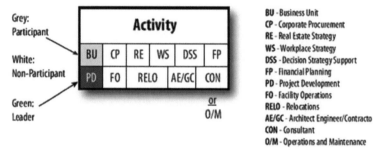

Figure 15: Activity Involvement Boxes (Lapinski, 2005)

However, in order to develop a true information flow plan (rather than a glorified workflow), the process map needs additional components, specifically: 1) the inputs, 2) outputs, 3) constraints or controls that bound the activity, and 4) mechanisms (people, tools, and techniques) that can be utilized for that activity (see Figure 16).

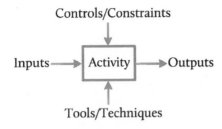

Figure 16: Information Flow Plan Components

People, Tools, and Techniques
Traditionally, much of the focus regarding process mapping gets placed on the inputs and outputs. As the previous chapters discussed, there are significant socio-technical factors that are specific to information flow. In terms of information flow planning, these have the greatest implications for tools (including people) and techniques that are utilized throughout the process.

People
Although innovative technologies get a lot of attention, collaboration will always center on bringing together a diverse group of *people* to accomplish a task that is too challenging for one person to tackle alone. The challenge is figuring out when and how best to involve the different individuals. In construction teams, involvement is typically defined by contracts, but most contracts are based on a very mechanistic view of project teams (i.e. that when a piece is plugged into the system, it automatically performs its function in concert with all the other moving parts). This perspective ignores almost all of the social and socio-technical characteristics that are so vital to information flow (value and mental model convergence, psychological safety, management of ambiguity, etc). To address this, project managers need to consider not only technical roles, but also how supporting roles and key

social roles required within the team throughout the delivery process.

Designers, contractors, and consultants often say that they want to be involved earlier in the delivery process. Yudelson and Fedrizi in their book "The Green Building Revolution" (2008) call this the 3E's of integrated design: you have to address Everything, with Everyone, Early. Why is this? First, earlier involvement of key team members provides an opportunity for everyone to get to know their fellow team members beyond their contractual role. By understanding the full spectrum of a person's technical knowledge (i.e. beyond just their contractual role), a team can identify unanticipated opportunities for synergies and innovation. Similarly, understanding a person's social role and work style can provide insight as to how they will energetically fit into the rest of the team, how they should be partnered with complementary team members, and what types of motivation will be most effective with them. Engaging key individuals earlier enables the project manager to understand more about them and how to incorporate them (and their potential information contributions) into the existing process more effectively. In addition, it provides time to adapt the information management plan based on these insights. Early involvement of key individuals also provides value to the individuals themselves. It provides them greater understanding of the intent and context for the project and allows them to offer innovative ideas and considerations before the team makes limiting decisions that render those options no longer viable.

Another important, but commonly overlooked, factor in planning information flow is the involvement of non-technical team members. Often, the team members who are brought in for their technical knowledge spend much of their time working on administrative issues such as figuring out how to use various tools or boundary objects, using them ineffectively, or making sure various boundary objects are properly maintained. While these tasks are necessary, they take away from those individuals' ability to focus on the more technical aspects of the project (i.e. why they were brought into the team in the first place). For this reason, it is important to incorporate into the information plan various supporting roles, especially where complicated tools and objects are used. These supporting roles can be provided by individuals already playing a technical role, but it is important that this be explicitly acknowledged and accounted for within the information flow plan as a part of their work load.

Some of the most critical supporting roles are the types of individuals described in Chapter 3: *Integrators*. Individuals with integrative competencies play a vital role in both facilitating social and technical integration and managing information flow within the team (especially in heavily collaborative portions of the process). They need to manage cycles of trust and learning so that the team environment is most conducive to information sharing, processing, and decision making. In the Chapter 3 discussion about the triggers that cause team dynamics to shift from negative to positive interactions, some of the important integrative competencies were mentioned; however, it is important to reiterate and elaborate upon them here. Specifically, these competencies are:

- *Appropriate breadth and depth of technical knowledge*, i.e. having a holistic understanding of the scope of work that they are integrating so that they can have substantive discussions with each specialist but also translate information into forms that are more relevant to others.
- *Social awareness and emotional intelligence*, i.e. being able to observe subtle signs of how team members are feeling and whether they understand relevant information so that they can take steps to adjust the current discussion and

interpersonal dynamic to create a more favorable environment and engagement of the full team.

- *Expectation management,* i.e. being able to effectively manage expectations to create the stable psychological environments required for higher-level learning and the development of trust.
- *Strategic use of tools and techniques,* i.e. being able to match tools with the appropriate dimensions to support discussions and being aware of how various tools and processes affect the facilitation of trust and learning so that they can be used strategically.
- *Translational thinking,* i.e. being able to help make connections between what one person says and what that implicitly means for others, similar to the way in which client goals need to be translated and linked to project team strategies; this requires that the integrator understands the various individuals' perspectives, act quickly, and think creatively.
- *Planning and dynamic capabilities* – an integrator needs to be able to develop detailed and comprehensive plans, but also be able to quickly adapt their plan based on changing situations.

The means and methods that integrators use to help facilitate collaboration are a vital component to influencing information flow in project teams. However, significant thought also has to be given to how information will be captured and disseminated to other technical groups and other phases of the project. This challenge of making sure that important information persists throughout the process requires the careful integration of boundary objects into the information flow plan as well.

Tools
Boundary objects are meant to complement the tacit knowledge provided by project team members, so it is

important to carefully and consciously evaluate and modify existing objects and consider developing new objects to support the information flow plan. Commonly we focus on boundary objects as tools that serve as repositories for information, analysis tools, or means of transferring information from one entity to another. However, certain boundary objects can also be used strategically to provide structure to team interactions and impose disciplined focus on certain types of information (i.e. the information needed for the object). In many ways, boundary objects, because of their clear and unchanging structure, can be used to more predictably plan the specific types of information and processes that are needed. Boundary objects can be used as:

- Sources of information (e.g. guides from industry sources, boundary objects from previous phases, etc.);
- A means to pull tacit information from project team members (e.g. models, sketches, or other objects that can capture at least one dimension of information above the common understanding);
- Repositories of information (e.g. databases, drawing sets, reports, etc.).

Objects that serve as sources of information and repositories of information are essentially the same thing. The only difference is that one is used to inform the team during their interaction (i.e. an input), while the other is a product of the interaction (i.e. an output).

To minimize process waste, project managers should start their planning with the objects that constitutes the final deliverables and work backward through the process to make sure that all preceding objects are capturing the right types of information and feed into what is needed to add value to the final product. While source/repository types of objects hold the inputs and outputs of an interaction, there are also objects that can be used during the interaction to pull tacit information from team members. These objects are tools that integrators can use to facilitate more effective interactions. In some cases, such as when teams used a building information model and modified it in real-time during the meeting, the same object can be used to pull information, capture it, and disseminate it. However, this relies on a very skilled boundary object manager to run the model proficiently during the meetings, maintain it outside of the meetings, and make sure that certain information gets disseminated to related objects or processes.

The types of boundary objects incorporated into a process also have an effect on the:

- Type of information that is readily available to the project team, i.e. information that is readily available is more likely to be used than information that requires extended searching;
- Type of questions being asked, i.e. information that is clearly missing from a structured format pulls that information from the team;
- Types of collaboration needed to further develop the object, i.e. whether the object is individually constructed, cooperatively constructed (i.e. different individuals are responsible for different parts), or collaboratively constructed (i.e. multiple individuals work together to develop the entire content).

As was mentioned in Chapter 1, boundary objects can also be characterized by their relationships with other objects. Specifically, they can be: 1) nested (i.e. several objects that feed into one master object), 2) linked (i.e. where different portions of the information in one object feeds into several others), or 3) coupled (i.e. where two objects capture basically the same information but from different responsible parties).

These types of object-to-object relationships can be used to make sure that important information is not lost, specifically: 1) linked relationships can be used to disseminate information from a particular scope group or a multidisciplinary coordination group to related groups, 2) nested relationships are needed toward the end of a phase when the various objects from different coordination groups need to be combined into a master object, 3) coupled relationships are needed to transition from one phase to another, i.e. one object is the product of the previous phase and the other establishes the intent for the next phase, 4) linked relationships are also needed to break the major intent object for a phase into the subsections that each scope needs to consider, and 5) the whole cycle repeats itself. Figure 17 illustrates this cycle within the context of the typical design and construction phases of a project.

Another means of using boundary objects to manage information throughout a process is to organize them by their level of abstraction. Important scopes of information should have four types of objects associated with them: 1) intent objects that provide an overview of the goals and overarching guidance with respect to a specific scope of information, 2) product description objects that provide a detailed description of the final product, 3) process description objects that provide a detailed description of the process needed to realize the final product, and 4) validation objects that provide a means for making sure that the final product satisfies the original intent.

Finally, there are also management issues associated with boundary objects. These are issues related to ensuring that the various boundary objects for different phases are used as effectively as possible. As was previously noted, one of these is making sure that complex objects have managers in order to reduce the administrative burden on the rest of the team so that they can focus on providing valuable technical knowledge. Another issue is making sure that the boundary objects being used during a specific set of activities have enough dimensions to support or guide the discussion. Finally, there is often a question regarding whether it is worthwhile to develop project-specific objects or use ones from past projects. Greater understanding of how an object will be used (i.e. through developing a plan) makes it easier for project teams to decide whether to adopt existing objects, modify existing objects, or create new custom objects.

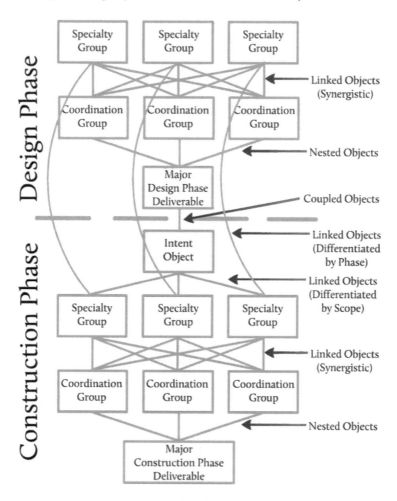

Figure 17: Interrelation of Boundary Objects

Another means of using boundary objects to manage information throughout a process is to organize them by their level of abstraction. Important scopes of information should have four types of objects associated with them: 1) intent objects that provide an overview of the goals and overarching guidance with respect to a specific scope of information, 2) product description objects that provide a detailed description of the final product, 3) process description objects that provide a detailed description of the process needed to realize the final product, and 4) validation objects that provide a means for making sure that the final product satisfies the original intent.

Finally, there are also management issues associated with boundary objects. These are issues related to ensuring that the various boundary objects for different phases are used as effectively as possible. As was previously noted, one of these is making sure that complex objects have managers in order to reduce the administrative burden on the rest of the team so that they can focus on providing valuable technical knowledge. Another issue is making sure that the boundary objects being used during a specific set of activities have enough dimensions to support or guide the discussion. Finally, there is often a question regarding whether it is worthwhile to develop project-specific objects or use ones from past projects. Greater understanding of how an object will be used (i.e. through developing a plan) makes it easier for project teams to decide whether to adopt existing objects, modify existing objects, or create new custom objects.

Techniques

The third important component that needs to be considered in developing an information flow plan is the techniques or "micro-processes" that can be used to search for, analyze, and disseminate information as well as making decisions. The process mapping techniques outlined earlier in this chapter can be a valuable tool for evaluating existing processes or developing new and innovative parts of a process. However, the complexity and interrelation of activities increase exponentially as the maps get into finer levels of detail, making it unrealistic for most projects to efficiently plan beyond the second or third level of detail. Instead, information flow managers can develop a suite of "micro-processes" or generalized techniques that can be repeatedly applied to various situations. By focusing on developing these techniques, managers and project teams can become proficient at them and reap the benefits sooner than if every step in a delivery process were customized. Repeatedly use of the same set of techniques also adds an element of expectation management and consistent work rhythms are established which further improves the quality of information and results in smoother flow.

For example, by becoming proficient at a handful of generic creativity-focused processes, production-focused processes, and validation-focused processes, teams can simplify their work flows while increasing their effectiveness.

Creativity-focused processes are designed to pull unfiltered information, innovative ideas, and spontaneous collaboration from the project team. One creativity-focused technique could be brainstorming (i.e. a short period of rapid-fire, free-flowing ideas shared by all team members without judgment or evaluation and resulting in a large amount of ideas clearly visible to the team). The goal of brainstorming is to create a situation where an idea by one person stimulates additional ideas by others so numerous good ideas are collaboratively generated in a short period of time without anyone claiming any one idea as their own. However, brainstorming alone is not very effective. The precursors and follow-up activities are just as important as the actual brainstorming. Prior to the brainstorm, it is important to: 1) clearly define the intent of the activity (i.e. the goal of the session), 2) clarify personal goals, biases, and concerns, and 3) define the constraints, timeline, process, and expectations of the session. These activities help to establish the "creative space" (or bound the brainstorming) so that any ideas that emerge within that space are relevant. If done interactively with full participation, the brainstorming process also helps to get the team comfortable sharing their ideas and thoughts with the group and helps to ensure collective buy-in to the results. Following the brainstorm, it is critical to categorize and order the mass of ideas so that a handful of clear and feasible options can be identified and pursued further. This step takes discipline, but is where brainstorming provides real value to the project. Finally, there should be a clear understanding of the next steps needed to further develop the most promising options so that decisions can be made in the future. All together these activities establish a technique that can be used numerous times throughout all stages of a project (see Figure 18).

Creativity-Focused Processes

Figure 18: Generic Creativity-Focused Process

The beauty of perfecting this type of general process is that a manager can utilize it whenever they need to conduct a quick, multi-disciplinary search for information regarding a specific issue. A manager who is proficient at conducting these brainstorming sessions can get them down so that they require no more than 15 minutes total.

Similarly, project managers can develop *production-focused processes* geared toward processing large amounts of data (e.g. creating drawing sets, conducting repetitive analyses, documenting as-built conditions). Although most people's tendency is to jump in and start producing the actual data, from an information flow effectiveness standpoint it is also necessary to: 1) first define the process (i.e. the process itself, the roles and responsibilities, and the deliverables); 2) Evaluate the process with the individual involved to gain buy-in, facilitate trust through transparency, enable learning regarding timing of involvement and interdependencies, and evaluate the process for comprehensiveness; 3) run the actual process; and 4) review the process after a few iterations to provide feedback and for continuous improvement (see Figure 19). These additional steps address subtle ambiguity and inefficiencies that individually may not seem significant, but can compound over several iterations and add significant waste to the process.

Production-Focused Processes

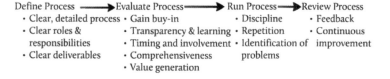

Figure 19: Generic Production-Focused Process

Finally, *validation-focused processes* are essentially decision-making processes. They are used to evaluate various options and arrive at the best decision for the project. These types of processes can take many forms, but having a well-thought out and explicitly stated process for validation always improves the quality of the information and builds trust among the team by demonstrating fairness and transparency (e.g. Figure 20). Because of multiple variables, their interrelation, and other intangible factors, many decisions in construction projects cannot be reduced to a simple computation. However, by tying everything back to the project goals and related metrics, following a known and stated process, and being open about personal biases, conflicts can be discussed openly and fairly and are less likely to result in affective conflict within the team.

Validation-Focused Processes

Figure 20: Generic Validation-Focused Process

Process Checks
The goal of information flow planning is to combine the right people, tools, and techniques so that the conditions are optimal for the right information to flow at the right time. Once teams have developed an information flow plan for their project, there are some basic checks that managers can run to evaluate their plan, identify problems, and address any problems in a timely manner. These checks may include the following:

Ambiguity Management Checks
- Clear Goals Check – Are there clear goals at each stage of the plan that tie directly to the overall project goals? Are these goals explicitly stated and communicated to the team?
- Clear Approach Check – Is each step in the process clear and relatively free from ambiguity in interpretation?
- Clear Roles Check – Is each individual's role and the responsibilities associated with that role clear for each activity? Are there means for holding individuals accountable for their performance related to their role?

Lean Process Management Checks

- Feedback Check – Are there means built in to the process to help identify problems when they arise? The sooner that problems are identified, the less impact they will have on the team's outcome. Often problems only become apparent when deliverables fall short of expectations. By having "mini-deliverables" for each activity, teams can identify problems almost immediately rather than allowing them to compound until they are discovered at major deliverables. Managers should build time into the process for identifying problems and solving problems.

- Pull Check – Is everything that is being done really needed? All activities should be focused on generating value for the project. By starting with the desired outcome and working backward through the process, managers can evaluate whether each step in the process actually is required to provide an output that is needed for subsequent activities.

- Workload Leveling Check – Can team members realistically meet their responsibilities (e.g. timing and quality)? Where is more time or additional support needed? Are technical individuals also accounting for any supporting activities that they are expected to perform? Despite the typical overly optimistic expectations, approximately 50% of work plans are actually completed on time (Ballard and Howell 2003). The weak points and bottlenecks in the workflows that cause these delays affect related areas and result in major waste to the project. Methodologies such as the Last Planner System seek to improve this by gaining realistic commitments from the responsible parties (i.e. the foreman in the field rather than the project manager in the office). In addition, through detailed information flow planning, many of these potential problems can be proactively identified and managed more carefully.

Socio-Technical Integration Checks

- Boundary Object Integration Check – Are the individual, cooperative, and collaborative boundary objects linked, nested, or coupled in a way that makes sense? Are the right types of objects being used for the right types of processes? Are there redundant boundary objects or objects that can be combined? Does it make sense to create custom objects for certain parts of the project?

- Expectation Management Filter – Do team members know what is expected of them and by when? For example, often at big coordination meetings individuals come to the meeting but are not sure of what specifically will be discussed, what the critical issues are, or what information they will need to provide. In the information flow plan, are "pre-meetings" included in the process so that individuals know what will be expected of them at the meeting and can come prepared to share the right information and evaluate information from others? Will the people capable of making decisions be present? Regularly scheduled meetings can provide a level of expectation management by following a known format and consistently holding individuals accountable for their responsibilities, but one-time meetings should include some element of formal preparation.

- Development of Trust and Learning Check – Are team members involved early enough to establish needed levels of trust and common understanding? Information flows differ from labor and materials flows in that "just-in-time" production does not work. Providing and processing information requires an element of psychological safety, so it is important that teams or individuals who are new to a team have time to develop basic levels of trust and a common understanding prior to the points when certain critical information is needed from them. In addition, learning (especially double-loop learning) requires some processing time so it may be necessary to give individual more time to process and understand big ideas.

- Buy-in and Commitment Check – Are individuals who need to commit to a decision given the opportunity to be part of the development of the options being considered? In most cases, individuals do not actually care if they "get their way" regarding certain decisions as they feel that they were heard and taken seriously. Although these individuals suggested certain ideas that were decided against, they were usually happy to pursue the alternate options as long as they fully understood why their idea was not selected. Taking time to explain decisions and solicit buy-in is one of those things that may seem unnecessary, but is necessary to ensure that individuals will continue to share important information and that decisions are meaningful and sustainable.

Whereas understanding the structure, characteristics, and moderators of information flow is essential to making sure that valuable information is made available, information flow planning is essential to making sure that that information adds value to the project. By developing information flow plans focused on selecting the appropriate strategies that provide value to the end user and strategically integrating the right people, tools, techniques, and process checks, our industry will take a major step towards giving information flow management the level of attention that has been lacking. However, efficient implementation of these plans goes beyond a bunch of boxes and arrows. Our industry needs to develop leaders and exceptional people who realize the tremendous potential of developing information flow management into a science and a practice. Along with leadership, we also need to develop the complementary organizational structures and strategies to support trust-based, learning-focused project team environments.

Chapter 6

Managing the Project Team Culture

The last aspect of information flow management has to do with managing the overall context within which project teams operate. As far as context goes, construction projects are a very unique and complex situation. In their seminal study, Lawrence and Lorsch (1967) found that as complexity increases, there is greater need for specialization. However, they also found that with greater specialization, there is also a greater need for integration. For the last few decades the design and construction industry have done a very good job with the specialization part. Our contracts, organizational structures, and strategies all are based on a highly specialized and differentiated project environment. However, until recently, we have sorely neglected the necessary complementary integration (and the resulting negative effects to our industry have reached a critical mass). Fortunately, integration is very much a buzzword in today's project teams. However, it is nearly impossible to really integrate within a system without understanding the context in which that system exists.

With construction teams, there are five main factors that define context:

- Industry environment;
- Organizational structures of individual parent companies involved with the project;

- Organizational structure of the project team;

- Organizational strategy of parent companies;

- Organizational strategy of the project team.

Industry Environment
Though there have been numerous studies identifying the important technical and social environmental characteristics that influence teams and organizations, the most critical technical characteristics are:

- *Complexity or diversity*, i.e. the number of elements that need to be dealt with simultaneously;

- *Uncertainty or unpredictability*, i.e. the variability of the conditions or ability to predict outcomes;

- *Interdependence*, i.e. the extent to which the work products and processes are interrelated (Scott and Davis, 2003; p. 126).

Galbraith (1977) proposed that the amount of information that needs to be processed in order to execute a task is directly dependent on these three environmental characteristics. However, when several of these characteristics are present, they result in a much greater influence on information needs, i.e. Complexity x Uncertainty x Interdependence = Task Information Requirements (Scott and Davis, 2003; 129).

In the construction industry, most projects are a perfect storm of technical requirements that place extremely high information requirements on project teams. In terms of complexity, construction teams are extremely diverse. Most teams consist of dozens of specialties that make up the temporary organization that is responsible for collectively delivering an entire building. There are often over 30 different firms and several hundred individuals involved with a single project (e.g. contractors, designers, consultants, etc.) and even individuals from the same company may have different functional backgrounds, breadth of experience, and individual goals. In addition to the diversity of the organization, there is also complexity resulting from the fluid participation of individuals. As the project progresses, different firms are brought into the project and others leave or decrease their participation. Even within the context of a single firm there are different individuals involved in different capacities throughout the various phases (e.g. for architects, one individual may come up with the concept, another is responsible for developing the technical details, and yet another does the construction administration). Furthermore, there is the complexity related to the uniqueness of the project: not only is each building unique, but the makeup of the team, the market conditions, the site conditions, and the combination of products, processes, and roles and responsibilities are different from any past project.

Construction project teams have to deal with large amounts of uncertainty. The environment surrounding construction projects is extremely dynamic. The markets for materials, labor, and the buildings themselves are subject to a host of factors such as the amount of construction ongoing in the area, the sophistication of the design and construction professionals, commodities markets, seasonal issues, regional issues, weather, local regulations, financial policy, etc. In order to navigate these factors, it becomes necessary for project teams to survey and forecast environmental conditions and take appropriate steps to prepare for their anticipated effects. Additionally, there are constantly new products, management and construction techniques, software, and other technologies that come onto the market and need to be understood by teams. These innovations require firms to figure out what effect these new products and processes have on design, construction, and building performance. In some cases, as with building information modeling (BIM) and sustainability, these innovative ideas require the development of new skills and create new functional areas. Finally, there are seasonal and weather issues (fuel prices, rainy seasons, low temperatures, ground freezing, etc.), local regulations (e.g. permitting processes, codes, etc.), and regional issues (e.g. familiarity with certain materials, availability of options) that can create additional uncertainty if not well understood.

In terms of interdependence, it was already mentioned that most projects involve 30 or more different firms and hundreds of individuals. On complex projects, the number of firms can be upward of 50 or 60. The multi-disciplinary nature of these types of teams requires close coordination between different scope areas, between the various phases of the project, and between each of the individuals on the project team and their parent company. All these factors together make construction projects extremely complex, uncertain, and interdependent and therefore require the processing of a tremendous amount of information.

The combination of high complexity, high uncertainty, and high interdependence makes the technical requirements (i.e. the *amount* of information that needs to be processed by construction teams) extremely high. However, there are several social characteristics of the environment that also influence information behaviors within teams, specifically: 1) *Comprehensiveness* (i.e. the acceptable level of search/research), 2) *Attitudes toward risk* (i.e. willingness to take on risk and pursue innovation), and 3) *Attitudes toward others* (i.e. the inherent level of trust). These characteristics affect the way that teams search for, accept, and capture information, respectively. Again, the construction industry faces significant challenges with each.

One critical factor for construction teams is that members rely almost exclusively on the knowledge and experience from past projects. There is very little searching for new knowledge from industry sources, academic publications, and other outside sources. Most projects rely almost solely on the first-hand and second-hand experience of the project team members and their ability to interpret and apply those experiences to the current project. In their study of construction teams, Hanlon and Sanvido (1995) found that 81% of information on projects comes from tacit knowledge. Consequently, "information searching" on projects is primarily limited to directly asking other project team members or individuals back at one's parent company. There is relatively little research of explicit sources of information. One challenge with relying on tacit knowledge is that it comes from a collection of unique situations that have their own specific characteristics and circumstances that make it difficult to generalize or directly apply to another unique project. The other challenge is that, for individuals who have no history of working together, it is difficult to evaluate the validity of an individual's "opinion" as opposed to "factual" information published by a mutually respected source (e.g. a national organization). This heavy reliance on the tacit knowledge of the team also makes it difficult to become aware of and incorporate academic research or aggregated best practices into a project. The advent of building information modeling is one promising area where academic findings are being eagerly sought and incorporated into practice. However, an added challenge is that most projects are heavily constrained in terms of budget and schedule, so there is the perception that there is no time or money available for research or more comprehensive searching (despite the downstream efficiencies and benefits that may result from that search).

Risk aversity and low initial trust between team members stem from the nature of these teams as a collection of individuals are only working together briefly and still have their primary allegiance to their parent firm. Individuals involved in construction projects have a unique situation where they are simultaneously involved with two organizations. They are members of their parent firm (e.g. architecture firm or contracting firm) as well as the temporary organization that is formed to deliver the project (i.e. project team). This dual allegiance can result in conflicting interests depending on their levels of commitment to each organization. In most cases, the major factor affecting an individual's commitment toward either organization is the level of alignment between the individual's personal goals and values and those of the organization. Another aspect of construction projects is that certain team members are heavily involved and responsible for certain phases, but much less involved (or not involved) in other phases (e.g. an architect is in charge of the design phase, but has much less authority and influence in the construction phase). These shifts related to power, ideology, and intensity of effort affect an individual's commitment to the project throughout the various phases.

In terms of attitudes toward risk, the construction industry is notoriously risk-averse when it comes to innovation. Due to the strong schedule and budget pressures on project teams, individuals are much more likely to use the same processes, strategies, and tools that they have used before rather than try something new. Most teams have a preference for accepting inefficiencies that come from dealing with *known* problems rather than the *unknown* problems that may come from pursuing innovations that could be much more effective. Traditional contracts also discourage innovation by rewarding each entity for how well they perform their specialized scope of work regardless of how it affects other scopes. Although there may be ideas that result in better outcomes for the project, individuals are very resistant to do anything differently than what they have done in the past because of the risk that it may reduce their efficiency. Another factor that exacerbates risk aversion on projects is that individuals are rewarded by their parent firm and not by the project team, so their performance is evaluated based on what matters most to their parent firm.

Finally, construction projects are characterized by very low levels of initial trust. Part of this is due to the fact that these are relatively short-term collaborations with each entity holding separate contracts, so there is little incentive to develop deeper relationships or risk the vulnerability that is required to build trust. Another factor is that most project team members have a fixed contract amount. This causes them to be very defensive about scope creep or picking up the slack for others. Lastly, a major contributor to this low trust environment is the threat of litigation. Our industry has become so preoccupied with assigning blame for any failures in performance that we have created countless formal processes to officially document every questions, comment, and decision. For example, on a recent project a contractor submitted a formal request for information (RFI) regarding a structural question. The structural engineer responded formally to the RFI by stating that "the RFI was inappropriate (period)". The contractor then called the structural engineer to make sure that she understood the question, to which she responded that she understood the question perfectly and even knew the answer, but that she wouldn't provide any information until the RFI officially referred to an approved detail in the drawing set and stated why the detail was not sufficient. Why? If she had responded to the RFI as it had been written, then it could have been construed that her answer was directing the contractor to deviate from the approved detail, whereas if the contractor first referenced the detail then they are instigating the deviation. All that fuss over a piece of rebar.

There are many factors that influence the project environment, but the most important are: 1) the *technical* characteristics of a) complexity, b) uncertainty, and c) interdependence; and 2) the *social* characteristics related to a) comprehensiveness of information searching, b) attitudes toward risk, and c) inherent trust and willingness to collaborate. Environment, however, is only part of the greater project context. The corresponding organizational structures and strategies in place are just as critical.

Organizational Structures

Each of these environmental factors has implications for the organizational structures that are best suited for that specific case. Complexity and interdependence require both a greater need for greater specialization and a greater need to effectively integrate those specialized scopes of information. Uncertainty, on the other hand, requires flexibility and adaptability in dealing with changes and making decisions. Therefore, one means of evaluating various organizational structures is to look at how they enable: 1) specialization; 2) communication between specialties; 3) decision-making; and 4) adaptation to the existing structure. The most prevalent types of organizational structures are: functional hierarchy, multidivisional, and matrix structures. There are also types of structures, such as markets, networks, and "adhocracies" (which are described subsequently), that are in some ways more representative of temporary organizations that result from multi-firm collaborations. Each of these structures addresses the challenges of specialization, communication, decision-making, and adaptation in different ways.

Functional hierarchies are based on grouping individuals with similar skills in the same unit (see Figure 21). These individuals usually have highly specialized and formalized work roles that allow them to become highly adept at their specific role but also makes it easy to interchange them with another similarly trained individual. Functional hierarchies tend to be best suited for organizations with a focus on one main core technology. Communication flows through long-looped vertical channels with progress reports and explanations flowing up and directives and instructions flowing down. In order to communicate with other units, communications need to essentially travel far enough up the hierarchy until they reach the level where an individual oversees both units. Because of the high level of formalization, coordination is mostly accomplished through simple means such as standard procedures and scheduling. Decision-making is controlled by executives at the top of the hierarchy. Since these types of organizations are designed for stable and repetitive environments, they may notice slight deviations from their structured processes very quickly but are not able to easily adjust to changes.

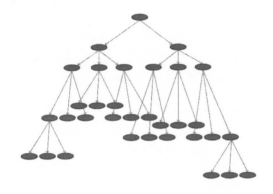

Figure 21: Functional Hierarchy Structure

Multidivisional structures are based on projects rather than functional area (see Figure 22). These types of organizations place different types of resources in a single self-contained unit (i.e. each division that is responsible for the design, marketing, fabrication, accounting, etc. of a single product). Each unit is focused on addressing the full spectrum of needs for a specific project. Communication tends to consist of short horizontal feedback loops that stay within the unit. The coordination mechanisms between divisions tend to be more complex because they require coordinators and liaisons to other groups. Most of the decisions are made by the unit, whereas executives are mainly concerned only with the results rather than the day-to-day operations. Because of the multi-disciplinary nature of the unit and the shorter communication lines, these types of organizations can respond more quickly to changes in the environment when they occur. However, they are often less aware of potential problems because they are focused mainly on their specific division and not on surveying the overall environment.

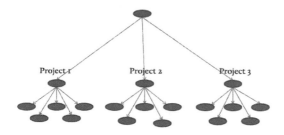

Figure 22: Multidivisional Structure

Matrix organizations are essentially a hybrid of functional hierarchies and multidivisional product-based organizations (see Figure 23). Individuals simultaneously specialize in their functional area and are concerned with its application to a specific project. While this can provide more effective communication between product divisions through the functional groups, it also requires that individuals manage both types of coordination mechanisms (i.e. simple and complex). Decision-making can also be complicated as each individual reports to both a division leader and a functional leader. In terms of adapting to change, matrix organizations can either reap the benefits of both functional and multidivisional structures (i.e. quick detection of potential problems and quick adaptation), or they can fall victim to the limitations of both (i.e. slow adaptation and poor detection).

The critical factor in the success of matrix organizations is how they balance their functional versus divisional tendencies.

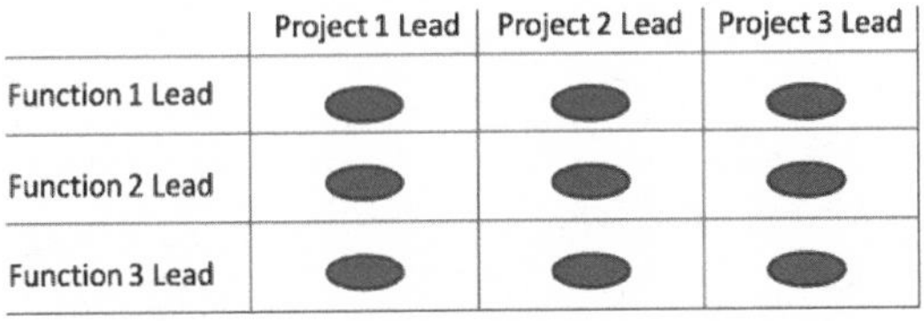

	Project 1 Lead	Project 2 Lead	Project 3 Lead
Function 1 Lead	⬭	⬭	⬭
Function 2 Lead	⬭	⬭	⬭
Function 3 Lead	⬭	⬭	⬭

Figure 23: Matrix Structure

Structures such as functional hierarchies, multidivisional, or matrix organizations tend to work well for collaboration within a single firm or other longer-term relationships, but are too structured to enable many different firms to effectively integrate their roles and workflows. Instead, for shorter-term collaborations between firms, organizational structures such as markets, networks, and adhocracies provide more relevant insight into these types of situations.

Markets are non-structured forms (see Figure 24). Instead of having a pre-defined structure, markets result from spontaneous coordination based on the self-interested actions of individuals and firms; for example, volatile supply/demand driven systems such as the stock market, negotiable marketplaces, and to a lesser degree construction products and other commodity markets. Specialization is based on the maturity of the market and usually stems from one firm trying to differentiate itself from the others. Markets create an environment well-suited for fast, simple communication and coordination, but are not as conducive to meaningful integration. While markets are open to everyone and offer choice, flexibility, and opportunity, they only allow for limited personal involvement and do not establish strong bonds between entities. As a result, markets are poor devices for learning and the transfer of technological know-how (Powell 1990). Decision-making in markets is highly dependent on prices. The nature of markets makes adaptation to the environment almost instantaneous. However, there is little consideration regarding the long-term wisdom and direction of their adaptation, and they tend to be too fast-paced and fleeting for meaningful collaboration.

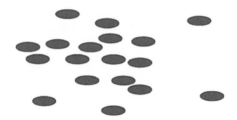

Figure 24: Markets

Networks are based on network theory, in which transactions occur through a web of individuals engaged in reciprocal, preferential, mutually supportive actions (see Figure 25). The basic assumption in network theory is that each entity is dependent on the resources controlled by others in the network and that by pooling their collective resources everyone can benefit. Essentially, each entity agrees to forgo its right to pursue its own interests at the expense of others so that both risks and rewards are shared. Networks also rely heavily on exchanges of roughly equivalent value or unbalanced exchanges coupled with indebtedness and obligation that reinforce the connections between firms.

In networks, each entity is defined both by its specialty, but more importantly how its specialty is related to the other specialties in the network. The importance of each role is not determined by hierarchy, but instead by how much it benefits the others in the network. As the firms in networks collaborate, they develop a mutual orientation and begin to understand and share goals (Powell 1990). This open-ended, relational nature of networks allows for the flow of "thicker" information than markets allow and "freer" flow of information than hierarchies allow (Kaneko & Imai 1987). Decision-making is based on negotiation between network members with each entity's respective influence being determined by its links to others. Their complex but informal communication paths allow for fast access to information, flexibility, and responsiveness to changes. Networks also can allow for many of the same benefits of vertically integrated organization (e.g. improved coordination, economies of scale, risk reduction through supply chain management) without the negative side effects of structural inertia and slow response times.

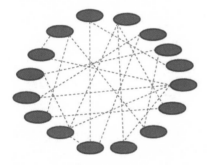

Figure 25: Representation of a Network

Adhocracies, on the other hand, are based on systems theory. Proponents of systems theory strive to improve organizational design by looking at multiple variables simultaneously (i.e. work flows, control systems, information processing, planning mechanisms, knowledge transfer, and the complex interactions between all these aspects). Because of the complexity of these relationships, these systems cannot be described using conventional models and therefore need to be simulated or observed in reality to try to understand their behavior. The branch of systems theory that attempts to explain these complex systems is "chaos" or "complexity" theory. This theory insists that "order emerges naturally because of unpredictable interactions" and that "chaos is the source of creativity and construction in social dynamics" (Marion, 1999). Naturally, this makes the notion of an adhocracy a very nebulous and difficult to fully grasp (see Figure 26).

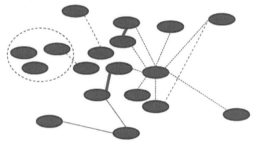

Figure 26: Representation of an Adhocracy

There are some characteristics that do hold true for most ad hoc organizational structures. Cohen, March, and Olsen (1972) and Weick (1969) described these types of organizational structures as "organized anarchies" and identify them by three prevalent characteristics: 1) problematic preferences, 2) unclear technology, and 3) fluid participation. The first characteristic is the notion of "problematic preferences" or the tendency to try to fit known products, systems, and methods to meet the project needs rather than developing project-specific solutions that are best suited for the given projects. The second characteristic, unclear technologies, refers to the tendency for individual firms to use their own processes and not really understand the processes of others involved in the temporary collaboration. Fluid participation is the third general characteristic and involves the constant shifting of boundaries, roles, importance, and involvement of entities.

Adhocracies have unique means of dealing with specialization, communication, decision making, and adaptation. The fluid participation makes specialization difficult because members vary in the amount of time and effort they devote to different domains. As a result the boundaries of the organization are uncertain and changing and therefore job descriptions are often ambiguous and overlapping. Communication also can be challenging because each entity usually uses its own processes and does not understand the processes used by other firms or take the time to develop common processes. Communication channels emerge organically through trial and error, learning from past experience and the path of least resistance. Decision-making also occurs somewhat haphazardly, as the audiences, power, distribution of power, and available solutions are constantly changing. In many cases, in an attempt to avoid conflict, decisions are often avoided, deferred, made by oversight, or never implemented. While adhocracies are constantly adapting to changes in the organizational makeup and the environment, they often lack a basic level of stability required for past decisions and overarching strategies to persist in a meaningful way.

Within a particular project, the project team rarely thinks of itself in terms of whether they are structured as a network, adhocracy, market, or other organized form. Instead, they rely on contractual arrangements and delivery methods to dictate the formal relationships between entities. These structures define the paths of communication within the project. For example, the most prevalent type of construction project delivery method is design-bid-build. In these types of projects, the owner holds a direct contract with the architect who in turn has direct contracts with the other design professionals and consultants. When the design is complete, various general contractors bid on the design and the selected contractor then holds a direct contract with the owner. The general contractor brings on subcontractors and contracts with them to perform specific scopes of work. If the plumbing subcontractor has a question during construction, it first has to go to the general contractor, then to the architect, then to the mechanical engineer. Once the mechanical engineer develops an answer, it is sent back to the architect to review, then to the general contractor, then finally back to the plumbing subcontractor who then needs to perform the work. This type of project structure is very similar to functional hierarchies, where formal communication runs in long vertical loops. Despite the formal communication paths dictated by this structure, there are often ad hoc informal communication loops that develop in order to short-circuit these long inefficient loops that cause the structure to resemble more of an adhocracy-hierarchy hybrid. This loose, nebulous understanding of how structure affects performance is precisely why the construction industry could gain some valuable insight from applying the work that has been done on organizational structures to their own contractual arrangements and delivery methods.

Other delivery methods may involve a construction manager (e.g. CM Agency or CM at Risk). In these cases, the CM is responsible for managing the project for the owner, but has varying levels of power depending on whether they are "at risk" (i.e. hold a contract with the owner and contracts with the architect and general contractor) or are merely an "agent" where they hold a contract with the owner, but the owner still holds the contracts with the architect and general contractor. More sophisticated owners who want to exercise greater control over the project may choose to utilize a multiple prime delivery method where the owner contracts directly with several of the major contractors to exercise greater control over the project. There are other variations on delivery methods, but traditionally the most common are Design-Bid-Build, CM Agency, CM at Risk, and Multi-Prime, which are for the most part hierarchy-based.

In the last 10-15 years, there has been a slow but growing trend toward more integrated delivery methods. One of these has been Design-Build. In design-build projects, the architect and general contractor form a single entity for the project. They are both under a single contract with the owner for the design and construction of the project. The joint accountability and early involvement of the contractor provide significant benefits to coordination. The challenge has been that the contractors are usually the ones with the bonding capacity large enough to secure the job, so the designers usually end up feeling like consultants to the general contractors. Although Design-Build projects have been shown to perform better in terms of quality, schedule, and cost, there have also been projects where the design has been greatly compromised in order to meet the schedule and budget. As a result of these occasional negative experiences, there is a general distrust and resistance to design-build within the design community.

In recent years, the notion of integrated project delivery (IPD) has gained popularity. In a general sense, IPD is thought of as a network of commitments. The way that the network is structured can vary, but essentially the major entities in the project team work as one unit with the risks and rewards shared between them. The American Institute of Architects outlined the basic principles of IPD as: 1) Mutual trust and respect; 2) Mutual benefit and reward; 3) Collaborative environment and decisions making; 4) Early involvement of key participants; 5) Early goal definition; 6) Intensified planning; 7) Open communication; 8) Appropriate technologies; and 9) Organization and leadership. Since IPD is more a mentality than an explicit delivery method, it has legal, contractual, and process components that can be incorporated into more traditional delivery methods. However, the true value of IPD can only be realized when holistically and whole-heartedly adopted by the project. Coincidentally, there are many characteristics of IPD that also make it an ideal environment for advanced information flow management.

Organizational Strategies

Whereas organization structure provides the *framework* for an organization to perform, strategy provides the *impetus* that drives that performance. Just as with structure, strategy can be discussed in terms of the parent firm or the project. Organizational strategy is different from the strategies discussed in the previous chapters. Here "strategy" refers to the overarching attitude or mindset of the organization or project team (e.g. related to innovation, openness, cost-control, etc.). Strategy can be viewed as a specific pattern in decision making or as a focus on specific key resources that provide a competitive advantage.

In terms of strategy as a pattern of decision making, there are several types of strategies that organizations tend to pursue. Miles and Snow (1978) describe three main strategy types: Defenders, Prospectors, and Analyzers. Each differs in the way that it deals with three theoretical problems: 1) the entreprenuerial problem (i.e. the fit between their product and market), 2) the engineering problem (i.e. selection of the appropriate technologies), and 3) the administrative problem (i.e. implemention of the processes needed for the organization to function and grow).

Defenders are organizations that focus on only a limited segment of the entire market. Typically, these segments are healthy and relatively stable. Managers tend to focus on efficiency in cost and quality. They also tend to not allocate many resources toward monitoring other organizations, events, or trends, but rather grow by penetrating deeper into their current markets through cautious, incremental growth. This is how defenders address their entreprenuerial problem. In terms of engineering, their focus is on producing and distributing their product as efficiently as possible (i.e. heavy reliance on cost-efficient technologies). They are likely to strive for vertical integration within their domain so that they can more efficiently control the flow of materials and cost throughout the entire production process. Regarding the administrative problem, these types of organizations tend to rely on centralized control with specialists grouped by similar skills and a high degree of formalization and codification of procedures and job descriptions. Because of their focus on cost effiency, the power in these organizations tends to lie with the financial and production experts. They also tend to use intensive planning that is oriented toward reactive problem solving (rather than problem finding).

Prospectors, on the other hand, focus on finding and exploiting new products and market opportunities. Since their domain is broad and constantly changing, they need to have significant resources dedicated to monitoring environmental conditions, trends, and market events. Their growth stems from finding new markets and developing new products. In terms of engineering, prospector organizations have a large portion of their resources devoted to production of prototypes and development of multiple technologies for each idea. Due to their need for flexibility, they embed the requisite skills and technologies in their people rather than routines or scripted processes. Administratively, their focus is on being able to deploy and coordinate resources between many decentralized units rather than exercising strict control. Therefore, they tend to have an adaptable, loosely fomalized structure that can rapidly respond to environmental changes. The main power centers revolve around marketing and research and development. They tend to use broad planning that is oriented toward problem finding and relies on feedback from experimental action.

Analyzers are those organizations that operate in two types of markets: one that is stable and another that is changing. They tend to identify and exploit new product/market opportunities while maintaining a stable core of products and client base. Therefore, they need to constantly monitor the actions of prospectors and select the best products and markets. Their growth comes from both penetrating deeper into existing markets and developing new products and markets. In terms of engineering, analyzers need to strike a balance between technological flexibility and stability. This tends to manifest itself through developing a dual technological core (i.e. both stable and flexible) that is based on a strong applied research group. This dual focus on stable and dynamic areas poses significant administrative challenges. Analyzer firms tend to have functional units that are centralized and budget-oriented in order to encourage cost-effectiveness in their stable areas, but also have project groups that are more results-oriented and focus on how new products can be adapted to existing technologies. The control in these types of organizations tends to lie mostly with marketing, applied research, and production. Since they are a mix of defender-like and prospector-like sub- groups, they rely on both intensive (i.e. detailed) and extensive (i.e. comprehensive) planning.

Miles and Snow also describe a fourth kind of organization, called "reactors" that are unstable organizations that lack a consistent strategy. This can be due to: 1) management's inability to articulate a clear organizational strategy, 2) having a clear strategy but not the appropriate technology, structure, and processes to support that strategy, or 3) adherence to a particular strategy and structure even though it is no longer relevant to the environmental conditions.

These general strategy descriptions consider strategy as patterns in decision-making and actions. Strategy can also be characterized as a focus on specific resources that provide a sustained competitive advantage. According to Barney (1991), what makes these resources a sustained competitive advantage is that they are: 1) valuable; 2) rare among the firm's current and potential competitors; 3) difficult to imitate; and 4) no strategically equivalent substitutes exist. When all four of these conditions exist, then organizations have the potential for a sustained competitive advantage.

While in some firms, there are highly secretive or patented technologies that provide a sustained competitive advantage, most firms in the AEC industry rely on the tacit knowledge embodied by their personnel for their competitive advantage. The collective knowledge and competencies of the people in a firm create a valuable, rare, non-imitable, and unique resource that, if properly cultivated, can provide a powerful and sustainable competitive advantage. For this reason, it is worth looking deeper at some learning and knowledge-based strategies.

Learning and Knowledge-Based Stategies
In developing strategies for organizational learning, it is important to understand the drivers for learning. Paul Shrivastava (1983) pulled together a typology of learning organizations based on research by others and identified the major causes of learning as: 1) a response to changes in the environment (e.g. Cyert & March, 1963); 2) a function of better understanding others' perspectives (e.g. Argyris & Schon, 1978); 3) a result of better understanding potential options and their potential range of outcomes (e.g. Duncan & Weiss, 1978); 4) insights gained from repetition (i.e. the experience curve); and 5) knowledge gained from research and development (Powell et al., 1996).
Shrivastava also goes on to classify six different types of learning systems that develop within organizations as a result of the causes outlines above. These consist of:

1) A single person who acts as peak coordinator and is knowledgeable about all aspects of the business (Mintzberg, 1979);
2) Perpetuated stories that develop into organizational myths;
3) Information seeking cultures;

4) Participative learning systems (e.g. creation of ad hoc committees);
5) Formal management systems;
6) Bureaucratic learning systems (e.g. corporate training programs).

These systems vary in terms of whether they operate at the individual level (system 1), group level (systems 2 and 4), or organizational level (systems 3, 5, and 6). They also vary in terms of whether they evolve organically (i.e. systems 1-3) or are designed and imposed upon the organization (i.e. systems 4-6). The appropriate system for a given firm is largely dependent on the culture and competencies that already exist within the firm.

In addition to understanding the causes of learning and the types of organizational learning systems, it is also important to understand the was in which learning can be leveraged: specifically, exploitation and exploration (Benner and Tushman, 2003). Exploitation involves a local search for new information that builds on the firm's existing technological capabilities (i.e. incrementally improving and building upon existing knowledge). Exploration, on the other hand, involves a more widespread search for new capabilities (e.g. radical change). A simple analogy is to think of is trying to improve upon the ladder: exploitation is trying to develop a better ladder, while exploration is coming up with the elevator. Exploitation is less risky, but only allows for incremental improvement. With a concerted focus on learning, a firm with an exploitation-based strategy can steadily work its way down the experience curve and increase the output to effort ratio (see Figure 27). Exploitative learning strategies have the most profound implications early on because that is when firms can double their output to effort ratio most quickly (Leiberman 1984). Exploration, on the other hand, may result in the development of a whole new learning curve (see Figure 21).

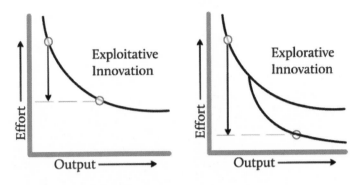

Figure 27: Learning Curves for Exploitative and Explorative Innovation

There is also the school of thought based on the idea that "the more you know, the faster you can learn". Cohen and Levinthal (1990) proposed the notion of *absorptive capacity* that essentially states that the more a firm already knows, the more easily and effectively it can evaluate and utilize new knowledge. Prior knowledge enables firms to recognize the value of new information, understand the best way to integrate it into existing operations, and market it to clients. This mimics individual learning which depends on association (i.e. linkages of new information with pre-existing concepts). While this makes a strong case for the value of a diverse workforce, Cohen and Levinthal also warn that there is a fine balance that needs to be struck in terms of diversity; there needs to be enough diversity to facilitate the sort of learning and problem solving that enables innovation, but also enough knowledge overlap to ensure effective communication.

One of the major challenges with developing organizational strategies and implementing learning systems is that they often take several years to develop or evolve. So what happens on project teams where individuals from different firms are brought together for a relatively short period of time?

First of all, strategy on construction projects varies tremendously. Part of the challenge is that every project is made up of different people from different firms and everyone has a way of doing things with which they are comfortable and proficient. Another factor is that every owner has a different level of sophistication in terms of design and construction and therefore may either have strong opinions and a clear plan for how things should be done, or they may have very little idea and leave it to the architect and general contractor to dictate that strategy. Lastly, there are also characteristics of the market environment that influence strategy such as industry trends, the level of competitiveness and sophistication of the firms that could be involved, and availability of critical resources or materials. Most projects strategies tend to fall into one of three categories: 1) haphazardly emergent, 2) mandated by the client/owner, or 3) thoughtfully emergent.

The majority of projects tend to fall into the haphazardly emergent strategy category. There is no formal planning that goes into developing the project strategy; rather, it tends to follow the general pattern of past projects and tends to change as the primary players running the project change. For example, in the design phase the project tends to mirror strategies that design firms have used on past projects. In the construction phase, the strategy shifts as the general contractor takes over much of the leadership, but there is still influence from the architects. Likewise, any other influential or charismatic individuals from key engineering or consulting firms may also influence the overall strategy. The type of contract (e.g. lump sum, cost+fee, unit cost, best value, guaranteed maximum price, etc.) also influences project strategy because it creates different attitudes toward risk, efficiency, and innovation. Therefore, the resulting strategy ends up being influenced by the project team members, delivery method, and contract type.

One way to overcome this haphazard, socially-constructed, turbulent project strategy is to establish very clear and distinct goals. Goals are usually mandated by the owner, but occasionally come from either the architect or general contractor. Especially with a fairly sophisticated owner, these goals can be clearly stated and interwoven into the process through contract language, the basis of design, and constant reiteration from the owner's representative to the project to create a consistent pattern in decision-making. For example, when the Santa Monica Freeway was damaged after the 1994 Northridge Earthquake, the contractor was given a $200,000 per day early completion bonus because the most critical goal was to get the road up and running as soon as possible. This clear goal was interwoven into the contract so that schedule considerations were the dominant factor in all decisions and any strategies that improved the schedule were explored thoroughly.

Most projects, however, are not as straightforward as the rebuilding of the Santa Monica Freeway. Most projects have several goals that need to be considered simultaneously and most project teams have certain strategies that they are most familiar with and proficient at executing. Ideally, the project team should develop a custom strategy for their project based on the capabilities and goals of each project team member and find a way to align those with the goals of the overall project. However, other than some very progressive projects, this thoughtfully emergent project strategy is currently far from the norm.

Though there is a lot of debate regarding which of the three factors (environment, structure, or strategy) is the primary influence governing the others, there is an overwhelming consensus that misalignment between the three results in poor performance. The pervasive problems that the construction industry has faced for the last half a century suggest a significant misalignment.

Environment, organizational structure, and organizational strategy are very broad areas of study. While there is a long tradition of comprehensive research programs by world-renowned organizational scientists in these areas, the construction industry has largely ignored or is unaware of these valuable insights. Part of the challenge is that our industry is different from the typical organizations that provide goods or services. Our industry is based on relatively short-term collaborations between dozens of different entities with the purpose of delivering a complex one-of-a-kind product. Because of this notable difference, applying the findings from the organizational sciences and best practices from other business sectors can be a challenge. However, the bigger challenge for the construction industry is that we do not have a detailed understanding of our own structures, strategies, and environment. This lack of understanding makes it difficult to identify opportunities to adopt research findings and innovations from other sectors.

Chapter 7

The Path Forward

The architecture, engineering, and construction (AEC) industry has suffered from stagnation over the last half century. While productivity in other industries has more than quadrupled over the last fifty years, construction productivity has actually declined. A large part of the problem is that we have developed systems, structures, and processes that foster defensive protectionist behavior and adversity to risk and innovation. The result has been that we find ourselves overwhelmed by information that we cannot manage, coordinate, or integrate and subsequently end up with a tremendous amount of untapped potential. So how do we address our industry's performance problems holistically? Specifically, how do we change the way that we collaborate in teams, the way that our project teams integrate information into a project, and the way that our projects inform and respond to the AEC industry at large?

The short answer is that we need to improve the flow of information on our projects. The more complex answer is that we need to fundamentally re-evaluate the way that we do work by: 1) gaining a better understanding of what we actually do; 2) developing the competencies, tools, and processes needed to improve the ways that we work together; 3) using knowledge of the social, technical, and technological characteristics of our industry to develop holistic, comprehensive information flow plans and practices; and finally 4) adapting our organizational structures and strategies to create the type of trust-based, learning-focused environment that we need in order to deliver the great buildings of the future.

We are at a crossroads in our industry's development. The economic crisis of the last few years has hit the construction industry especially hard. While for some it has meant layoffs, downsizing, or closing up shop altogether, for others it has provided a much needed opportunity to carefully re-evaluate our priorities, make thoughtful strategic decisions about our future, and begin a transformation that will better enable us to tackle the challenges of a new era.

Along with these opportunities, there have also been a few trends that, if embraced and developed fully, provide tremendous promise for transforming our industry. The first is sustainability. Sustainable design is not a new concept, but over the last decade it has really taken a hold in the mainstream consciousness. Real sustainable design and construction (as opposed to the superficial only-for-marketing-purposes variety) requires that we develop a deep understanding of how buildings perform and how we can integrate various systems to work in harmony with each other and the surrounding environment. It has also forced us to evaluate our decisions not only in terms of economic first cost, but also in terms of life-cycle cost, environmental cost, and cost to society. It has influenced the way that we manufacture products, approach design, measure the success of our construction practices, and caused individuals that never interacted previously to have to collaborate. While the main selling point of sustainability has been to help the environment, it has also helped our industry by inadvertently requiring us to develop a greater understanding of the interrelation of design, construction, and performance and to take a vested interest in the success of others on the project team.

The second trend is the growing adoption of building information modeling (BIM). BIM has revolutionized the coordination process between design, construction, and operation. By combining the cost and schedule information with a three-dimensional representation of the project, it has been possible for the cost and schedule implications of design changes to be realized in real time. In addition, by developing the design in three dimensions, it makes the interdependencies and conflicts between components immediately apparent forcing even more collaboration. Software developers have developed platforms for different individuals to work on their individual models, upload them to a common coordination model, and run clash detection. Project teams can essentially build a virtual building before they build the actual building, enabling them to proactively address problems, identify opportunities for innovation, and improve coordination. While these developments have changed the way that designers and contractors understand their scopes of work and coordinate with others, these models also have the potential to be used in post-occupancy as facilities management tools. The beauty of BIM is that it can serve as a master boundary object that stays with the project from early design all the way through the life of the project and potentially also through the life of the building. The collaborative creation of building information models demands greater commitment, transparency in information sharing, and accountability for the quality of the model from all those involved. Finally, because the model can be reviewed in real-time, it enables everyone to develop a common understanding about certain conditions and also enables learning as the effects of changes can instantaneously be understood.

The third trend is the gradual acceptance of more integrated delivery methods, such as design-build and formal IPD. While our industry has been bashful about fully embracing these integrated delivery methods (as is witnessed by prevalence of design-assist and "IPD-lite" contracts), when fully embraced, they create project environments ripe for trust and learning. They align project goals with individual goals and enable close interaction of designers and contractors throughout the entire project so that they can better understand the perspectives, potential value, and concerns of the other. An increasingly prevalent sight on IPD projects is the creation of huge project trailers where all members of the team co-locate in a common office space throughout design and construction. This provides a much greater opportunity for social and technical integration and the development of informal structures and processes that organically emerge to address the specific needs of the project. Lastly, the substantive relationships that result from these types of projects help to increase our trust in one another and our collective commitment to improving our industry one project at a time.

The reason that these trends provide so much promise for our industry is that they are all subtly pushing us toward a more trust-based, learning-focused team environment that is essential for effective information flow. Quite simply, they are consciously and subconsciously forcing us to create the structures, strategies, and practices that we need to survive in today's changing world.

If these trends are a subtle hint nudging us in the right direction, this book is intended to be a big, blinking neon sign. The ideas in this book just scratch the surface. Whether we like it or not, we are living in a fast-paced, globalized, information-intensive world. Industries that cannot adapt to meet the challenges of this new age will fail. Those that can adapt will flourish. Despite the hype and allure of technology, it is not a panacea. In the construction industry, our biggest asset has been, is, and will always be *our people*. Therefore, anything short of a new paradigm that holistically addresses the social, technical, and technological aspects of our industry is not good enough.

At a personal level, we need to become more aware of our own behaviors through the lens of information flow and how they affect the success of the project. At an interpersonal level, we need to realize the importance of developing integrative competencies within our project managers so that they can better manage teams. At the project level, we need to elevate information flow planning to its own science and practice so that we can continue to further our understanding and improve upon our implementation of these techniques. Finally, at the industry level, we need to develop the appropriate structures, strategies, and priorities to support this new paradigm based on trust and learning.

The value of these notions extends beyond simply improving project outcomes. They also have significant implications for our industry at large and collaboration with the construction research community. There is tremendous potential that can come from carefully planned translational research between the construction industry and the wealth of knowledge that already exists within the organizational sciences and information sciences. In addition, academia can help address the pervasive deficiencies in our industry's knowledge base that continuously plague our project teams. However, leveraging these opportunities relies on close coordination between industry and academia in the form of data collection from existing projects, feedback on research, and a willingness to implement research findings on future projects. This has already begun as the findings from BIM and lean construction research in universities across the country are eagerly being sought by firms looking to become leaders in this new era.

Although the academic community is there to provide supplemental new ideas and innovation through research, it is also the responsibility of industry to continuously seek ways to improve the industry. By better understanding the science and practice of information flow management and integration, we can better utilize the tremendous *knowledge, creativity,* and *passion* that exist within the AEC industry. Specifically, looking at our processes, tools, and behaviors through the socio-technical lens of information flow management, we can:

- Developing long-term meaningful relationships with strategic partners and integrated our processes to collaboratively improve our holistic offering to our communities.
- More fully leveraging innovation into our existing practices so that we can deliver greater value with greater effectiveness and efficiency.
- Develop a genuine and committed practice of self-reflection and continuous growth/learning so that we are continuously identifying weaknesses that need to be addressed and responding to new needs.

So where does this leave us? The challenges of tomorrow are very real and a force to be reckoned with. How will the construction industry respond? Will we turn a blind eye and stubbornly hold fast to the outdated, ineffective practices that have resulted in the pervasive problems facing our industry? Or can we find a better way that turns this crisis into an opportunity for transformation into something better?

I challenge us to make this an opportunity to create the kind of industry that we really want, need, and deserve. Let us create a new paradigm focused on information and knowledge management, built on practices focused on trust and learning, and solely dedicated to helping us realize the greatness of our collective potential. After all, at the most fundamental level, this is what construction has been and should always be: The bringing together of different things and integrating them in such a way that the final product is worth so much more than the sum of its parts.

References

Allen, N. J., & Meyer, J. P. (1996). "Affective, continuance, and normative commitment to the organization: An examination of construct validity." *Journal of Vocational Behavior*, **49,** 252–276.

Argyris, C. and D. A. Schon (1978). *Organizational Learning: A Theory of Action Perspective*. Addison- Wesley, Reading, MA.
Ashforth, B.E. & Mael, F. (1989). Social identity theory and the organization. Academy of Management Review, 14, 20-39.

Axelrod, R.M. (Ed.) (1976). *Structure of decisions: The cognitive maps of political elites.* Princeton, NJ: Princeton University Press.

Ballard, G. & Howell, G. A. (2003) "Lean project management." *Building Research & Information* 31(2): 119-133.

Bandura, A. (1977). *Social Learning Theory*, Englewood Cliffs, NJ: Prentice Hall.

Barney, J. B. (1991). "Firm resources and sustained competitive advantage", *Journal of Management*, 17, pp. 99-120.

Barrick, M. R., Mount, M. K., & Judge, T. A. (2001). "Personality and performance at the beginning of the new millennium: What do we know and where do we go next?" *International Journal of Selection and Assessment*, 9, 9–30.

Benner, M. J., & Tushman, M. L. (2003). "Exploitation, exploration, and process management: The productivity dilemma revisited." *Academy of Management Review*, 28: 238–256.

CIFE. (Nov. 22, 2007). CIFE Technical Report, URL http://cife.stanford.edu/Publications/index.html

Cohen, W.M. and Levinthal, D.A. (1990). "Absorptive Capacity: A New Perspective on Learning and Innovation." *Administrative Science Quarterly*, Vol. 35: 128-152.

Cohen, M.D., March, J.G. and Olsen, J.P. (1972). "A garbage can model of organizational choice." *Administrative Science Quarterly* 17:1-25.

Cyert, R.M. and March, J.G. (1963). *A behavioral theory of the firm.* Englewood Cliffs, NJ: Prentice Hall.
Davis, T. R. V., & Luthans, F. (1980). "A social learning approach to organizational behavior." *Academy of Management Review*, 5. 281-290.

Dearborn, R., and Simon, H. (1958). "Selective Perceptions in Executives" *Sociometry*, 21, pp. 140-144

Dirks, K.T. & Ferrin, D.L. (2001). "The Role of Trust in Organizational Settings." *Organization Science*, Vol. 12, 450-467

Dirks, K.T. & McLean Parks, J.T. (2003) "Conflicting stories: The state of the science of conflict." In J. Greenberg (Ed.) *Organizational Behavior: The State of the Science 2nd Edition*, Mahwah, NJ. Erlbaum.

Duncan, R. B., & Weiss, A. (1979). "Organizational learning: Implications for organizational design." In B. Staw (Ed.), *Research in organizational behavior* (pp. 75-123). Greenwich, CT: JAI Press.

Earley, E.C. & Moskowski, E. (2000). "Creating hybrid team cultures: An empirical test of transnational team functioning." *Academy of Management Journal*, 43, 26-39.

Eisenberger, R., Huntington, R., Hutchison, S., & Sowa, D. (1986). "Perceived organizational support." *Journal of Applied Psychology*, **71,** 500–507.

Eisenhardt, K., J. Martin. (2000). Dynamic capabilities: What are they? *Strategic Management J.* 21 1105–1121.

Ellemers, N. & Rink, F. (2005). "Identity in work groups: The beneficial and detrimental consequences of multiple identities and group norms for collaboration and group performance." In E. Lawler (Ed.), *Advances in Group Processes. Vol 2,* p. 1-41, New York: Elsevier Press.

Fiol, C.M. and Lyles, M.A. (1985) Organizational Learning. *The Academy of Management Review*, Vol. 10, No. 4: pp. 803-813

Fiske, S.T., and Taylor, S.E. (1984) *Social Cognition.* Reading, MA: Addison-Wesley.

Follett, M.P. (1941). *Dynamic Administration: The Collected Papers of Mary Parker Follett.* Henry C. Metcalf and L. Urwick (Eds.) London: Pitman.

Folger, R., & Bies, R.J. (1989). "Managerial Responsibilities and procedural justice." *Employee Responsibilities and Rights Journal*, 2: 79-90.

Fong, G.T., and Markus, H. (1982). "Self-Schema and Judgments about Others." *Social Cognition*, 1, 191-205

Galbraith, J. R. (1973). *Designing complex organizations.* Reading, MA: Addison-Wesley.

Gardner, H. (1983) *Frames of Mind: The Theory of Multiple Intelligences,* New York: Basic Books

George, J. M. & Zhou, J. (2001). "When openness to experience and conscientiousness are related to creative behavior: an interactional approach." *Journal of Applied Psychology*, 86, 513–524.

Goode, W.J. (1960). "A Theory of Role Strain." *American Sociological Review*, 25, 483-496

Hambrick, D.C., Finkelstien, S., and Mooney, A.C. (2005). "Executive Demands: New Insights for Explained Strategic Decisions and Leader Behaviors." *Academy of Management Journal*, Vol. 30, No. 3: 472-491.

Hambrick, D.C. and Mason, P.A. (1984). "Upper Echelons: The Organization as a Reflection of its Top Managers." *Academy of Management Review*, Vol. 9, No. 2: 193-206.

Hanlon, E. and Sanvido, V. (1995). "Constructability Information classification scheme." *Journal of Construction Engineering and Management*, Vol. 121, No. 4, 337-345.

Hartley, J. (1998) *Learning and Studying: A Research Perspective*, London: Routledge

Hernes, H. (1997). "Crosscutting identifications in organizations." In S. Sackmann (red.) *Cultural complexity in organizations. Inherent contrasts and contradictions.* London: Sage, 343-366.

Holmes, J.G. & Rempel, J.K. (1989). "Trust in close relationships." In C. Hendrick (Ed.), *Close Relationships* (pp. 187-220). Thousand Oaks, CA: Sage.

Horman, M. J., Riley, D.R., Lapinski, A.R. , Korkmaz, S., Pulaski, M. H., Magent, C., Luo, Y. , Harding, N. , Dahl, P. K. (2006). "Delivering green buildings: Process improvements for sustainable construction," *Journal of Green Bldg.*, 1(1): 123-140.

Jehn, K. (1994). "Enhancing effectiveness: An investigation of advantages and disadvantages of value-based intragroup conflict." *International Journal of Conflict Management*, 5, 223-238.

Jehn, K. (1995). "A multimethod examination of the benefits and detriments of intragroup conflict." *Administrative Science Quarterly*, 40, 256-282.

Jehn, K. (1997). "A quantitative analysis of conflict types and dimensions in organizational groups." *Administrative Science Quarterly*, 42, 530-557.

Jehn, K., Chadwick, C., & Thatcher, M. (1997). "The agree or not to agree: The effects of value congruence, individual demographic dissimilarity, and conflict on workgroup outcomes." *International Journal of Conflict Management*, 8, 287-305.

Jehn, K.A., Northcraft, G.B., and Neale, M.A. (1999). "Why differences make a difference: A field study of diversity, conflict, and performance in workgroups." *Administrative Science Quarterly*, 44: 741-763

Jehn, K. & Mannix, E. (2001). "The dynamic nature of conflict: A longitudinal study of intragroup conflict and performance." *Academy of Management Journal*, 44, 238-251.

Kaneko, I. and Imai, K. (1987). "A network view of the firm". *1st Hitotsubashi–Stanford Conference, Tokyo, March 29–April 1*.

Kimberly, J.R. and Evanisko, M.J. (1981). "Organizational innovation: The influence of individual, organizational, and contextual factors on hospital adoption of technological and administrative innovations." *Academy of Management Journal*, 24: 689-713.

Koch, J.L. and Steers, R.M. (1976). "Job Attachment, Satisfaction, and Turnover among Public Employees." *Technical Report No.* 6, Office of Naval Research, University of Oregon.

Konchar, M. and Sanvido, V. (1998). "Comparison of U.S. Project Delivery Systems." *Journal of Construction Engineering and Management,* Vol.124, No. 6, 435-444

Kramer RM, Brewer MB, Hanna B. (1996). "Collective trust and collective action in organizations: the decision to trust as a social decision." In R.M. Kramer & T.R. Tyler (Eds.), *Trust in organizations: Frontier of theory and research*: 357-389. Thousand Oaks, CA: Sage

Lapinski, A. (2005), "*Delivering Sustainability: Mapping Toyota Motor Sales Corporate Facility Delivery Process.*" M.S. Thesis, The Pennsylvania State University, State College, PA.

Lave, J. and Wenger, E. (1991). *Situated Learning. Legitimate Peripheral Participation*, Cambridge: University of Cambridge Press.

Lawrence, P.R. and Lorsch, J.W. (1967). "Differentiation and Integration in Complex Organizations." *Administrative Science Quarterly*, Vol. 12, No. 1: 1-47

Lieberman, M. B. (1984). "The learning curve and pricing in the chemical processing industries," *Rand Journal of Economics,* vol. I 5, pp. 2 I 3-28.

Lord, R.G., and Foti, R.J. (1986). "Schema Theories, Information Processing, and Organizational Behavior." In H.P. Sims and D.A. Gioia (Eds.) *The Thinking Organization*, San Francisco, C.A.: Jossey-Bass, p.20-48

Lovelace, K., Shapiro, D., & Weingart, L. (2001). "Maximizing cross-functional new product teams' innovativeness and constraint adherence: A conflict communications perspective." *Academy of Management Journal*, 44, 779-793.

Marion, R. (1999). *"The Edge of Organization: Chaos and Complexity Theories of Formal Social Systems."* Thousand Oaks, CA: Sage

Merriam, S. and Caffarella (1991). *Learning in Adulthood. A comprehensive guide*, San Francisco: Jossey-Bass

Meyer, J.P., and Allen, N.J. (1991). "A three-component conceptualization of organizational commitment." *Human Resource Management Review*, 1, 61-89

Meyer, J.P., Stanley, D.J., Herscovitch, L., and Topolnytsky, L. (2002). "Affective, continuance, and normative commitment to the organization: A meta-analysis of antecedents, correlates, and consequences." *Journal of Vocational Behavior*, 61, 20-52

Meyer, J. P., Becker, T. E., & Van Dick, R. (2006). "Social identities and commitments at work: Toward an integrative model." *Journal of Organizational Behavior, 27,* 665–683.

Miles, R.E. and Snow, C.C. (1978). *Organizational Strategy, Structure, and Process.* New York: McGraw-Hill.

Mischel, W. (1977). "The interaction of person and situation." In D. Magnusson & N.S. Endler (Eds.), *Personality at the crossroads: Current Issues in Interactional Psychology*: 166-207. Hillsdale, NJ: Lawrence Erlbaum Associates

Mowday, Richard T., Lyman W. Porter, and Robert Dubin (1974) "Unit performance, situational factors, and employee attitudes In spatially separated work units." *Organizational Behavior and Human Performance*, 12: 231 -248.

Nissen, M. E. (2006a). "Dynamic Knowledge Patterns to Inform Design: A Field Study of Knowledge Stocks and Flows in an Extreme Organization." *Journal of Management Information Systems*, 22, 3, 225-263.

Nissen, M.E. (2006b). *Harnessing Knowledge Dynamics: Principled Organizational Knowing & Learning*. Hershey, PA: Idea Group Publishing.

O'Reilly, C. A. and J. Chatman. 1986. "Organizational Commitment and Psychological Attachment: The Effects of Compliance, Identification, and Internalization on Prosocial Behavior." *Journal of Applied Psychology 71: 492-499*.

Pelled, L., Eisenhardt, K., & Xin, K. (1999). "Exploring the black box: An analysis of work group diversity, conflict, and performance." *Administrative Science Quarterly*, 44, 1-28.

Polanyi, M. (1967). *The Tacit Dimension*. London: Routledge and Keoan Paul.

Pondy, L.R. (1967). "Organizational Conflict: Concepts and Models." *Administrative Science* Quarterly. 12: 296-320

Porter, L.W., Steers, R.M., Mowday, R.T., and Boulian, P.V. (1974). "Organizational commitment, job satisfaction, and turnover among psychiatric technicians." *Journal of Applied Psychology*, 59: 603-609.

Powell, W.W. (1990). "Neither Market nor Hierarchy: Network Forms of Organization." *Research in Organizational Behavior*, 12: 295-336

Powell, W.W., Koput, K.W., Smith-Doerr, L. (1996) "Interorganizational Collaboration and the Locus of

Innovation: Networks of Learning in Biotechnology." *Administrative Science Quarterly*, 41,1: 116-145.

Pulaski, M.H. and Horman, M.J. (2005) "Organizing Constructability Knowledge for Design" *Journal of Construction Engineering and Management*, ASCE August: 911-919

Robinson, S. (1996). "Trust and the breach of psychological contract." *Administrative Science Quarterly*, 41, 574-599.

Rousseau, D.M. (1995). "New Hire Perceptions of Their Own and Their Employer's Obligations: A Study of Psychological Contracts." *Journal of Organizational Behavior*, Vol. 11, No. 5. 389-400.

Rousseau, D.M., Sitkin, S.B., Burt, R.S., & Camerer, C. (1998). "Not so different after all: A cross-discipline view of trust." *Academy of Management Review*, 23, 393-404.

Saljo, R. (1979) "Learning about learning," *Higher Education*, no. 8, pp. 443–51.

Scott, W. R., & Davis, G. F. (2003). *Organizations and organizing: Rational, natural, and open systems perspectives.* Upper Saddle River, NJ: Prentice-Hall.

Shah, P. & Jehn, K. (1993). "Do friends perform better than acquaintances? The interaction of friendship, conflict, and task." *Group Decision and Negotiation*, 2, 149-165.

Shrivastava, P. (1983). "A Typology of Learning Organizations," *Journal of Management Studies*, 20, 2: 7-28

Simons, T., Pelled, L., & Smith, K. (1999). "Making use of difference: Diversity, debate and decision comprehensiveness in top management teams." *Academy of Management Journal*, 42, 662-673.

imons, T. & Peterson, R. (2000). "Task conflict and relationship conflict in top management teams: The pivotal role of intra-group trust." *Journal of Applied Psychology*, 85, 102-111.

Smith, M.K. (1999) "Learning theory", The Encyclopedia of Informal Education, www.infed.org/biblio/b-learn.htm (Last update: September 03, 2009)

Stacey, R.D. (2000). *Strategic Management & Organizational Dynamics.* Pearson Education Limited, Essex, England.

Tajfel, H. & Turner, J.C. (1986). "The social identity theory of intergroup behavior." In S. Worchel & W.G. Austing (Eds.), *The psychology of intergroup relations* (pp. 7-24). Chicago: Nelson-Hall.

Thoits, P.A. (1983). "Multiple Identities and Psychological Well-being: A Reformulation and Test of the Social Isolation Hypothesis." *American Sociological* Review, 48, 174-187

Tjosvold D. (1997). "Conflict within interdependence: its value for productivity and individuality." In *Using Conflict in Organizations,* De Dreu CKW, Van de Vliert E. (Eds). Sage: Thousand Oaks; 23-37

Tushman, M.L. (1977). "Special Boundary Roles in the Innovation Process." *Administrative Science Quarterly*, Vol. 22, No. 4., pp. 587-605.

Walton, R. & Dutton, J. (1969). "The management of interdepartmental conflict: A model and review." *Administrative Science Quarterly*, 14, 73-84.

Weick, K.E., (1969). *The Social Psychology of Organizing.* Reading, Mass.: Addison-Wesley

Wong, C., Tjovold, D., and Lee, F. (1992). "Managing conflict in a diverse work force: A Chinese perspective in North America." *Small Group Research*, 23, 302-321.

About the Author

Andreas Floros Phelps is an Integrated Projects Executive with the international construction firm Balfour Beatty. He works and lives in San Francisco, CA. His early professional years were spent developing a holistic understanding of building performance. This work with building science, design, construction, and failures investigations has given him a comprehensive understanding of how buildings behave and how design and construction processes directly and indirectly affect performance. As a technical consultant, he realized that construction industry has certain organizational and behavioral characteristics that make it difficult to fully integrate valuable new information into projects and therefore much of the potential value is often lost. This dilemma led him to pursue a doctorate in construction management at The Pennsylvania State University focused on understanding the interrelation of social, technical, and technological factors affecting information sharing, processing, and acceptance. This work has expanded to include information flow process planning, knowledge sharing and collaboration systems planning, and analysis of delivery methods in terms of their ability to promote trust and learning. His passion is finding new and innovative ways of understanding the construction industry and using that insight to help the industry continuously strive to realize its full collective potential.